"Two by Two"

The Shape of a Shapeless Movement

i

© Copyright 2013 Irvine Grey

Published in 2013 by
Irvine Grey
39 Calvertstown Road
Portadown
Northern Ireland
BT63 5NY

www.irvinegrey.com

Printed in Lisburn by Impression Print and Design NI Ltd.
Cover design and typesetting by Impression Print and Design NI Ltd.

ISBN 978-0-9575390-0-6

"Two by Two"

The Shape of a Shapeless Movement

A study of a religious movement started in Ireland in 1897 by
William Irvine and Edward Cooney

By
Irvine Grey

Table of Contents

Contents

Foreword

All sorts of exotic plants are found in the undergrowth of the religious garden, many of which seem to come from the species known as Evangelicalism. Among them is the tiny but intriguing plant that is known as the 2x2 movement. Irvine Grey has dug around and dug deep to expose the plant, which he was in part familiar with from his own personal experience, and has written a fascinating account of its origin, culture and doctrine.

The movement emerged in Ireland in 1897 under the inspiration of a Scot, William Irvine, who was soon joined by Edward Cooney from Enniskillen, although he later became suspect to succeeding leaders. The movement took its shape from Jesus' sending out of his disciples two by two, without material means of support, as reported in Matthew 10:1-5. In the early twentieth century it spread to other parts of the English-speaking world and claims to have around 600,000 followers.

Since it claims not to have any doctrinal foundations, eschews any name and affects not to have any organisation, the wonder is that it survives, let alone has had any impact. Operating on the fringes of evangelicalism, the movement came to claim that truth could only be found through the preaching of its itinerant workers which took place in its followers' homes, and which consistently demonstrated some very home-spun and fanciful interpretations of Scripture. Yet their workers did not preach anything which would be recognised as a commonly-accepted evangelical gospel and put forward no rationale for its emphasis on Matthew 10 to the exclusion of other patterns of mission found in the Bible.

Irvine Grey gives us the first in-depth analysis of the movement and the doctrinal foundation which it may deny it has but which nonetheless serves as the actual foundation of its work. He justly concludes that although it may try to shelter under the shade of Evangelicalism, its use of Scripture, approach to the Gospel, concept of mission and much else disqualifies it from being a true strain of Evangelicalism, even if it came originally from evangelical stock.

We tend to think of exotic new religious movements as recent. Sociologists often point to the efflorescence of new religious movements that blossomed from the counter-cultural of the 1970s. This shows that such a historical judgement is wide of the mark. But what amazes is the capacity of such movements, then as now, to attract followers to ideas that so transparently distort Scripture to their own ends – a sure sign that we are living, as Paul claimed, in the last period of history when 'some will abandon the faith and follow deceiving spirits...godless myths and old wives' tales' (1 Tim. 4:1-7).

This book is instructive on the 2x2 movement because it is carefully researched and comprehensively told. But it is also instructive as a warning not to take one part of Scripture and build a movement around it to the neglect of others, or foolishly to claim to be the sole possessors of truth that people need to 'profess', while condemning all others for error. 'Let anyone who has ears, hear...'

Dr Derek J Tidball, Leicester.

Dr Derek Tidball, a graduate in sociology from Durham University, a theology graduate from the University of London and with a Ph.D. from Keele University, is the former Principal of London School of Theology. He has previously chaired various national Evangelical organisations, including serving as Vice President of the Evangelical Alliance (UK).

Preface

Having read with interest the thesis '"Two by Two" – the Shape of a Shapeless Movement' it gives me great joy to write some words of endorsement. Growing up in County Fermanagh, as I did, in the fifties and sixties there were then two groups referred to as the "Cooneyites" and the "Reidites" and nothing of substance has been written about them and Irvine Grey is the person to fill this void. His maternal grandparents both 'professed' in a 2x2 mission in 1935 and his grandmother always looked upon that conversion as having changed her life.

Having graduated from Queen's University, Belfast with a Bachelor of Theology and with a Master of Arts from the University of Manchester, Irvine was well prepared, academically, to undertake this very readable research on the 2x2 movement.

Two sentences which end the thesis should be studied with care. 'This research has shown that the movement rejects central doctrines such as the Trinity, the deity of Christ and could not affirm the historical creeds. Therefore, the only reasonable conclusion one can reach is that the 2x2 movement is a cult and a particularly dangerous one.' All of Irvine's in-depth research uncovered the underlying beliefs and practices that led to his conclusion that the movement is a cult and particularly dangerous and deceptive.

I have known Irvine for fifty-five years and it is to his credit and enterprise that I can fully endorse his research and highly recommend it. Irvine has read all of the books available and critiqued them fairly. Particularly the book by Patricia Roberts, *'The Life and Ministry of Edward Cooney'* and uses some helpful information from it. Having read this book, I was disappointed with its tone and conclusions. She extols all of Cooney's views and supports his arguments!

The chief difficulty facing any researcher into this movement is that there are no records or books produced by the movement that outline the movement's mission and ministry. Since its inception in 1897 they have left no written records apart from their own hymnbook. Since their establishment over one hundred years ago their preachers and followers strongly resist associating with evangelical churches and believe that all are damned unless they hear the Gospel from a 2x2 preacher.

Irvine has been relentless in tracking the movement's views on the Bible, the Church, the Trinity, the Cross, the Gospel, conversion and many other important tenets of Christianity and finds that the 2x2s sit lightly on such major doctrines. I am sure that the 2x2 preachers and followers will reject Irvine's findings but it is my prayer that they will read it with an open mind and that the Holy Spirit will give wisdom and discernment to those who read it and that many will come out of darkness into the marvellous light of the Gospel of the Lord Jesus Christ.

Dr Herbert Boyd McGonigle, Manchester

Dr Herbert McGonigle is a graduate in divinity from the University of London, a Master of Arts from Leeds University and a Ph.D. from Keele University. He is the former Principal of the Nazarene Theological College, Manchester.

Commendation

This fine study of the nameless sect, the Two-by-Twos (2x2s) of the book, provides valuable information gathered by means of careful research and personal observation. It will be of great and lasting assistance to those seeking to identify the movement, which has been known by other names, for example "The Testimony" or "Christian Conventions". Although preachers claim that their movement has no name, and that it goes back to the time of Jesus Christ, Irvine Grey rightly discerns its nature as a cult of relatively modern origin, and shows the sect is a Christian deviation.

Preachers are sent to many countries but the movement has no written statement of faith, and no existent library of published material written by preachers. In spite of these limitations for the researcher, Mr. Grey has been able to make up-to-date observations on their teaching and practice, and has drawn upon members' comments to supplement research and sociological study. He has successfully brought shape to the detailed sketch of the house-church movement that has been achieved.

Similarly, the study of the movement's Irish history is informed by written testimony, conversations with members and preachers, and information collected from Mr. Grey's personal experiences of missions, home meetings and conventions held in Ireland and Stockholm, Sweden. It must be noted that Mr Grey is sensitive to the difficulties of active members, who strive to remain faithful to the workers' demands.

Theological discussion elucidates the unique characteristics that are integral to doctrine: preachers who go out two by two, and the church in the home. But of primary importance is the identification of the teaching on Jesus Christ as the Pattern Preacher who requires that His true followers take literally His injunction to the disciples in Matthew, chapter ten, to go out and preach, that is, to become homeless and poor. Mr. Grey argues that the emphasis upon preacher homelessness overshadows their view of the Divine Personhood of Jesus Christ, and shifts their teaching from the prevailing trend of Evangelicalism to that of a Christian deviation.

We warmly commend this book, which provides scholarly discussion on the identity and history, sociology and doctrine of the nameless house church.

Doug and Helen Parker, authors of *The Secret Sect.*

January 2013.

Acknowledgments

In reflecting upon how this research project began and progressed, I recognise that without the encouragement and practical support of others it would not have been completed. It is, therefore, with a real sense of gratitude that I place on record my indebtedness to them.

This has been a difficult project because of the lack of primary sources of information on the 2x2 movement and because they exist behind a veil of secrecy. I am deeply grateful to those overseers, workers and members who proffered assistance. Some for fear of reprisals, cannot be openly acknowledged.

It was my friend who is a fellow County Fermanagh man, Dr Herbert McGonigle, former principal of the Nazarene Theological College in Manchester, England with whom I first discussed the idea of this research project. He enthusiastically embraced the idea of researching the movement that had its roots in our home county and he remained a source of inspiration throughout. I thank him for writing the preface for this book. I am deeply indebted to former University of Manchester lecturer, Helen Susan Maclean for her valuable contribution to my research and her proof reading skills. I deeply appreciate the skill of Dr Philip Saunders who proof read the work and made some very helpful suggestions.

I am deeply grateful to my supervisor, Dr Maurice Dowling who with his accomplished skill and untiring patience guided me at every stage of my study. His insightful comments on my work always helped me to articulate my ideas more clearly. My other colleagues at the Irish Baptist College have also been a constant source of encouragement. Dr Ken Scott read the drafts of the thesis and his useful comments and suggestions reflect his genuine interest in the subject. I am also very grateful to Dr Hamilton Moore, former principal of the Irish Baptist College for his ongoing assistance and support. I commend the perseverance of Stuart Argue who spent many tedious hours transcribing sermons from 2x2 conventions and missions. The aid of college registrar, Valerie Hamilton was invaluable for her patient help in providing many reprints of the drafts and revisions of the thesis.

This project would never have seen the light of day had it not been for my mother, Mrs Elsie Grey. Her parents Robert and Minnie Crowe 'professed' at a 2x2 mission in 1935 when my mother was 12 years old. I will always appreciate the help she has been with information on the early years of the movement. Thanks mum for your love and interest.

I am deeply indebted to Dr Derek Tidball for writing the foreword. Dr Tidball, a former principal of the London School of Theology and the author of several books was interested in this work from the early stages and throughout my research.

Arguably the most influential and accurate assessment of the two by two movement came from Doug and Helen Parker in their book, *The Secret Sect* published in 1982. They are well equipped to critique any subsequent work on the movement and I am delighted that they have written a commendation of my research. To this wonderful couple I say a very sincere thank you not only for the commendation but for *The Secret Sect* that was so helpful throughout my research.

Finally, I want to express my deepest appreciation to my wife Ingvor and our family, Fiona, Lynda, David, Simon, their spouses and our five grandchildren. During the past four years I have devoted considerable time to researching, writing and re-writing this thesis and without your love, support and encouragement it would never have been completed.

Prologue

Little did I think that when I first enrolled as a part-time student at the Irish Baptist College in 2004 to study for a Queen's University theology degree, that I would eventually find myself embarking upon a research study of a religious movement that had fascinated me from when I was a young boy.

Growing up in County Fermanagh, Northern Ireland in the fifties one could not help but be aware of the presence of two religious groups that we euphemistically referred to as the "Cooneyites" – those who followed Edward Cooney after his excommunication from the movement in 1928. The others were known as the "Reidites" – because Wilson Reid was at one time the Irish overseer of what we now know as the 2x2 movement, although they still refuse to acknowledge any formal title.

The fact that my maternal grandparents and many of my close relatives were members of the 2x2 movement gave me a rare insight into something that was relatively obscure to outsiders. With my grandmother I attended the Fermanagh convention and even Sunday morning meetings, something I was never permitted to do during this research.

Our family attended Killadeas Methodist Church, the smallest Methodist Church in Ireland and it was there that I first heard the Gospel of Christ's saving grace just before my twelfth birthday and came to faith in Christ alone for my salvation. I was always close to my grandmother, being the first grandchild and in her words, 'you would really make a great worker.' But that was not to be. It was through these contacts that I met many 2x2 workers and was deeply puzzled by their exclusive claim that they alone could open the door to salvation.

It was my deep desire to establish what drives the 2x2 movement to that extent since their formation in 1897. They have left no written record of their history or beliefs and they reject any attempt by outsiders to seek to discover how they operate and what they believe. I embarked upon this research with an open mind, as far as I could tell and without any ulterior motives or preconceived ideas as to what I might discover. Since my research was governed by The Queen's University, this ensured the protection of participants and maintained public confidence in standards of the research and that it was conducted lawfully, with honesty and integrity, and in accordance with good practice.

This research was extensive and wide-ranging. With the lack of primary documents the information gathering required many hours of attendance at various missions and conventions as far away as Sweden. The three main sections - history, sociology and theology - were studied and critiqued separately with the emphasis on the theology of the movement.

My final conclusion as to where this movement stands theologically seemed the only reasonable conclusion possible. Any other conclusion would have betrayed the Scripture that clearly teaches that a person comes to faith in Christ through grace alone. There is nothing in Scripture to support an exclusive ministry of pairs of homeless preachers who meet only in homes or that one can come only to Christ through such a ministry.

I am sure that there will be those who will feel hurt by the conclusion of this research, but it is my prayer that the Holy Spirit will illuminate the truth of God's Word and that given the evidence unearthed, this research will lead many to Christ, the source of forgiveness, freedom and joy.

I have purposely published the entire thesis from pages 1 - 180 as it was presented to and examined by The Queen's University, Belfast, Northern Ireland.

Introduction

This study will focus on a new religious movement that commenced its activities in County Tipperary, Ireland in 1897. They eschew the idea of making a written record of any kind to explain their beginnings and beliefs. Therefore, we do not have access to any academic primary documents on the movement. Books that have been written over the years are by those who were once involved or by those who felt that they had sufficient knowledge of the movement to attempt an exposé of what they perceive as errors. These books mainly cast them in a negative light regarding their beliefs and practices.

Why Study This Movement?

Every religious group that lays claim to the label of Christianity contends that its beliefs and practices are biblical. It is, therefore, reasonable to examine any such group using their interpretation of Scripture as the criterion to establish if they are faithful to the meaning of the original text and traditional Christianity. The two by two (referred to as 2x2 in this thesis)[1] is a religious movement that asserts it has an unbroken link with the New Testament Church as established by the Lord Jesus Christ on the shores of Galilee. They have several hundred thousand[2] adherents worldwide with the main concentration in Ireland, the United Kingdom, the United States, Australia and New Zealand and a small presence in the West Indies and other countries. When asked what their doctrine is, adherents respond by pointing to the Bible and stating, 'this is our only doctrine'.[3] It is within the context of this claim that this study will examine the movement using the distinctively Scripture-based features of evangelical Christianity as the framework. Their history and sociology will form part of the study but the main emphasis will be on their theology. There will be an overlap in theological aspects, history and sociology. An important aspect will

---

[1]   The name being used for the movement in this research.
[2]   Estimates vary from 150,000 to 600,000.
[3]   Daniel, Kevin N, *Reinventing the Truth*, (Bend: Research and Information Services, 1993), 9.

be their interpretation of the Scriptures to justify their practices. The constant features in 2x2 preaching and discussions and the phrases that frequently occur are 'the Gospel' and 'the Truth'. They claim that salvation is only by hearing 'the truth'[4] from one of their workers.[5] The movement uses these two terms synonymously. Any attempt to understand their modus operandi is a difficult task and is confusing to outsiders. Many within the movement have little understanding of their beliefs and practices. For that reason, it is very appropriate to give as a title to this thesis, '"Two by two" – The Shape of a Shapeless Movement.'

The group refuses to take a name[6] and claims that like the early Christians they do not have a name. In the interests of continuity throughout this study, it is essential to use an appellation that best describes the movement. It is not my intention to thrust a name upon them but I feel it necessary to apply an epithet that I can use for the sake of both clarity and brevity. I have chosen the name 'Two by Two'[7] – hereafter referred to in this work, for the sake of brevity, as 2x2. A group that refuses to name itself usually finds that outsiders will then find a designation that can be wide ranging in application, such as the names of those who were the founding fathers or from practices associated with the group. The term 2x2 comes nearest to describing their ministry that they base on Matthew 10:5-15. An advertisement for their mission in 2010 in County Tyrone, Northern Ireland reads, 'conducted by the present day 2 BY 2 Apostles.'[8]

....

4   'The Truth' is a term that frequently occurs in their preaching and is used as a synonym for 'the Gospel' but lacks any clear definition. For a guide to the 2x2 terminology please see appendix 1, page 162.

5   They refer to their ministers as 'workers'. In 1903 the 'Living Witness Doctrine' became a tenet of the movement and teaches that no one can come to faith except through a worker. This is explained fully on page 31.

6   Their ministers have officially registered the group with various government agencies.

7   In a meeting on 20th January 2012 with Edgar Lowe, an Irish worker since 1979, he told how the term 'two by two' irritated him since the wording in the KJV, Mark 6:7 is 'two and two'. The wording is 'two by two' in the ESV, NIV and RSV.

8   Tyrone Constitution, 4th November 2010. The wording of this advertisement is significant in that the two workers are senior in the movement, Jack Duncan and Tommie Gamble, the overseer in Ireland. This appeared in subsequent advertisements for their mission in Lough Muck Orange hall. Missions in Orange halls and Masonic halls are common practice in Northern Ireland.

The founders of the 2x2s were William Irvine (1863 - 1948) and Edward Cooney (1867 - 1961). Since its inception, those outside the movement have called it by various names. These include the Irvinites and the Cooneyites but these are unsuitable since both Irvine and Cooney were excommunicated and the current 2x2s would prefer to deny connection with them. Irvine's departure was in 1914 followed by Cooney in 1928. 'Excommunicated' is not a term used by the 2x2s but the practice does exist within the movement. There is still a remnant who have remained loyal to Edward Cooney and his leadership although these would be small in number. Cooney's excommunication led to a split but the 2x2s emerged as the main group. Other names used in the past included 'The Dippers' and this was because of their practice of baptism by immersion in rivers, lakes or seas. The name, 'The Black Stockings', was used because the female members were required in those early days to wear black stockings. A name very familiar to me as I grew up in County Fermanagh in the late fifties and early sixties was simply 'The Meeting People' and this was because they met in homes and had no church buildings.

This work will examine the 2x2 movement but from time to time will refer to those who remained loyal to Cooney and in that context will use the term Cooneyite. Consultation of the 1911 Irish Census[9] shows that the entries of the early adherents of the movement list their religion as 'Christian' or 'information refused' in contrast to members of other denominations who clearly state their religious affiliation. Examples of this include the William West family, Mullaghmeen, County Fermanagh; against the name of each family member is 'information refused' but their servant, Annie Scott, is recorded as a Roman Catholic. In the 1901 census, this family was listed, some as Church of Ireland and some Methodist.[10] The Simpson family, Monea, County Fermanagh give their denomination as Methodist[11] in the 1901 census and in the 1911 census each member of the family is listed as

---

[9]   www.census.nationalarchives.ie. Accessed 28th January 2012. It is not possible to define actual numbers of 'information refused' responses.

[10] http://www.census.nationalarchives.ie/pages/1901/Fermanagh/Ballydoolagh/ Mullaghmeen/1363719/. Accessed 28th January 2012.

[11] http://www.census.nationalarchives.ie/pages/1901/Fermanagh/Monea/ Leighan/1362544/. Accessed 28th January 2012.

3

'Christian' but their boarder, William Armstrong, as a Presbyterian. This was quite usual for adherents of the movement.

Although the name 2x2 is widely used to identify them they do not accept this as their name. Both Irvine and Cooney were adamant that the Lord Jesus Christ in Matthew 10:5-15 sent the twelve out with explicit instructions as to how ministry should be modelled in the future and that meant that the apostles were sent out in twos, as homeless, itinerant ministers. On this short passage from Matthew's Gospel, they managed to establish a religious group that started in Ireland and now spans a large part of the world.

Although there are some books on the movement, there is no evidence that there has ever been an academic study carried out that embraces their history, sociology and theology. This study has been carried out by one who has observed the 2x2s over the past fifty years, but is not part of the movement.

Personal Experience

From boyhood, this movement has fascinated me for several reasons. Some of our immediate family were 2x2s, although this did not cause any particular dissension but often resulted in some lively discussions. My grandmother, Mrs Minnie Crowe, was undoubtedly devoted to the movement and an active participant in all of the meetings and conventions. Although my grandparents became part of the movement in 1935 when my mother would have been twelve years old, neither my mother, her sister nor two brothers ever joined the movement. In 1956, my father[12] granted two of their workers, Hugh Breen and Nat Stevenson, permission to erect a portable wooden hall in a field on our family farm in Killadeas, County Fermanagh, where they held a mission that lasted a few weeks.

The district in which we lived was a mix of families who were mainly Church of Ireland, Methodists and Roman Catholics. Our family worshipped in the Methodist Church and my father came in for heavy criticism from our neighbours for granting the ground for the mission. This was mainly because at that stage workers in the movement were openly highly critical of established churches and clergy. This led to major problems, especially when it came to burials since many of their members were buried in graveyards of established Protestant churches and I can recall several occasions when the local clergy refused the workers permission to speak at the graveside because of their belligerent attitude towards these churches.

In 1959, in the home of Mrs Sara West, Ballinamallard, I attended a meeting conducted by Edward Cooney and had an opportunity to talk with him. Mrs West and her husband John were early followers of Cooney and Irvine and it was on their farm in Crocknacrieve that they hosted the first convention in 1904.[13] John and Sara West with their daughter Ida were among those who continued in fellowship with

12 On reflection, I wonder if the 2x2s was targeting our family in a similar way that they targeted my grandparents' family in 1935 when after a mission on their farm they joined the movement.

13 I have deliberately not referred to this as a 2x2 convention since this was before the excommunication of Irvine and eventually Cooney in 1928 that led to the split.

Cooney following his excommunication.

When I was a teenager, my grandmother brought me along to the meetings and conventions and at that time, I could not see the significance of the exclusivity. Most of the studies and books on the movement have emanated from the United States. Because the movement has its origins in Ireland this study has the advantage of having immediate access to some who have been associated with the movement from the first half of the twentieth century. One senior worker from New Zealand made the comment, 'All things are not just as they are in Ireland and I'd like to contribute so that you get more than just an Irish perspective.'[14] This is a particularly significant comment in that this movement claims a worldwide continuity in their preaching and practices and this is obviously not the case.

[14]   Email 20th January 2012.

Methodology

On the premise that the 2x2 movement claims an unbroken link with the New Testament church and that their practices reflect this, the research will briefly examine the history and sociological aspects of the movement and comment on these before examination of their theology. This will include an examination of the Scriptures that the 2x2s use to support their *modus operandi*. The Bible will be the benchmark used for deciding whether their application of Scripture represents the doctrines of Christianity as formulated in the creeds[15] of the early church and if the movement represents the evangelicalism that McGrath describes as follows:

> *Evangelicalism is historic Christianity. Its beliefs correspond to the central doctrines of the Christian churches down through the ages, including the two most important doctrines of the patristic period: the doctrine of the 'two natures', human and divine, of Jesus Christ and the doctrine of the Trinity.*[16]

The four characteristics of classical evangelicalism were first outlined in 1989 by Bebbington who writes: 'variations there certainly have been in statements by Evangelicals about what they regard as basic. There is nevertheless a common core that has remained remarkably constant down the centuries. Conversionism, activism, biblicism and crucicentrism form the defining attributes of Evangelical religion.'[17] The basis for the conclusion reached in this research is on the framework of the four characteristics of classical evangelicalism.

These four characteristics are amongst the distinguishing marks of the New Testament church in the Book of Acts and they formed the basis of the Gospel for the early church. The 2x2 movement has never published anything apart from their own hymnbook and the absence

....

15   The movement has an intense dislike for any of the early church creeds, dismissing them as 'man-made'. This is somewhat of a paradox since they are at ease with using the hymns in their own hymnbook written by clergymen and others that they view as false prophets and hirelings.

16   McGrath, Alister, *Evangelicalism and the Future of Christianity*, (London: Hodder and Stoughton, 1993), 94.

17   Bebbington, David W, *Evangelicalism in Modern Britain*, (London: Unwin Hyman, 1989), 4.

of primary documents makes this research challenging. Reconstruction of their history will involve researching various archives including press reports dating back to the early days of the movement. A review of some of the books written by those who claim to know the movement and of some who have left the movement and tell their personal stories will help in understanding the movement's *modus operandi*. Cooperation from existing adherents should help give a balanced view of the movement and its activities.

Where it is possible and without compromising requests for confidentiality, the study will quote the views of leaders and members in the movement including those who are former members. My attendance as an observer at their gospel meetings and conventions will provide an insight to the content of their preaching and this should help build up a picture as to their theology. The two most emphasised distinctives of the movement are the church in the home and the ministry of homeless preachers who work in same-sex pairs.[18] These two distinctives feature frequently in 2x2 preaching and testimonies.

Examination of this movement which refuses to take a name will establish whether they can rightfully claim an unbroken link with the New Testament Church and whether it is truly evangelical in nature. Examination of the part that charismatic leadership may have had in starting this movement and how it maintains its position of exclusivity in the postmodern culture of the twenty-first century will form part of the study.

For over one hundred years, the religious movement that started in Ireland in 1897 has made claims that they and they alone are in possession of 'the truth' of Christianity and all other claimants are false witnesses. They believe that they alone represent 'the truth' as taught in the Bible - not just any Bible; it must be the King James Version, although there are indications that other versions are becoming acceptable, mainly the NIV and ESV.[19] In a general discussion with one of their mature members in Northern Ireland, I commented that I was researching their history to which his immediate response was, 'you

[18] Pairs of workers are referred to as companions.
[19] Worker email, 11th February 2012.

8

then will have to go back to the shores of Galilee.' A former member in the United States writes, 'when I was a young boy I was told by my mother and grandparents on several different occasions that the Truth was started by Jesus when he was here on Earth. . . . the impression I was left with was that the Truth had been in existence since Christ.'[20]

Another former 2x2, Cherie Kropp[21] who writes extensively about the movement states: 'For one thing, it was quite a surprise for me to find the "truth" has a founder and is not of apostolic succession as I had been told. My experience and reaction could be compared to a child discovering there was no Santa Claus.'[22]

The 2x2s teach that no one can know the gospel unless it is preached through one of their workers. The church in the home is the only form of weekly worship and this is for members only. They claim to have no formal structure or hierarchy. They keep no financial records; their workers have no visible means of support and the members provide food and accommodation. With no apparent formal organisation, the 2x2s manage to organise annual conventions in several locations virtually throughout the world with their workers in attendance, involving considerable travel expenses including airfares.

This research is following a similar method to that used by an earlier researcher, Keith Crow in his thesis, *The Invisible Church*. Crow states:

> *For reasons which may become more apparent later, I have not conducted formal interviews or collected questionnaires. The group, while not a "secret" sect, has a strong feeling that religion is a personal and private matter, and would be disturbed at being made an object of study. The sect abhors publicity of any kind. At any rate, it is my conviction that such data as might be gathered by these techniques would add little of value to the information I already have. Also, I have abandoned the convention that papers should be written entirely in the third person and without personal references. Its observation would have been both awkward and misleading.[23]*

---

20 Chapman, Daurelle, editor, *Reflections*, (Bend: Research and Information Services, 1993), 176.
21 Email, 30th December 2008.
22 Kropp's testimony in Chapman, *Reflections*, 397.
23 Crow, Keith W. *The Invisible Church*, A Thesis. This is a thesis written mainly from a sociology perspective presented to the Department of Sociology and the Graduate School of the University of Oregon in partial fulfilment of the requirements for the degree of Master of Arts, March 1961.

It seems highly unlikely there are any earthly movements that can truly lay claim to unbroken succession to the church founded by Jesus Christ and His apostles. This is a claim made by many movements over the centuries but on scrutiny, there is no evidence to support the claim. The view is widely held that the New Testament does not leave us with a particular model of ministry. Tidball contends:

> *That the New Testament writers set before us a number of models of ministry, each one of which is shaped by the needs of the church they were serving and no doubt, by their own individual personalities and interests as well. Each New Testament book has a lot to say about pastoral leadership, even if it is not apparent on the surface.*[24]

Daniel confirms that from the start of the movement, 'the "Workers"'[25] have taught, and most continue to assert, that the group is a direct, historical continuation of the "New Testament Church", having no earthly founder. This was first taught by the "early Workers", only in areas outside the United Kingdom and Ireland.'[26] Since their formation in 1897, they have failed to produce any written work, a creedal statement or a declaration of doctrine. As a result, there is almost[27] a complete absence of primary information from sources within the fellowship of this movement. There are numerous publications, books, pamphlets and websites and these provide an insight into their history, sociology and theology from others who were at one time members of the group and have written of their experiences. Where material from a website is used that needs permission this has been sought from the moderator.

To make this study as broad as possible, it will examine their history from the formation to the present day. The movement's sociology will form part of the study. Professor Steve Bruce,[28] School of Social Science, University of Aberdeen, suggested examination of how this

---

[24] Tidball, Derek, *Ministry by the Book*, (Nottingham: Apollos, 2008), 14.
[25] Worker is the name used for full time ministers in the movement.
[26] Daniel, *Reinventing the Truth*, 21.
[27] Two accounts do survive – a typewritten account of eighteen A4 pages by Goodhand Pattison in 1925 and a handwritten account of one hundred and ninety three pages by Alfred Trotter in 1968. Both men were in good standing in the movement.
[28] Email, 24th September 2008.

movement manages without any apparent formal organization; he asks, what are the criteria for membership of the 2x2s and how can they function without any apparent lines of accountability for members, workers and financial controls? According to Bryan Wilson, writing in the preface of *The Secret Sect*[29] this research confronts a formidable task:

> *The sociologist's intellectual curiosity concerning the way in which a movement such as the Cooneyites[30] maintains coordination and continuity, is complimentary to the historian's irritation that a body enjoying a strong sense of its own separated identity, with a shared conception of its purposes, mission and destiny should have persisted for three quarters of a century without leaving more trace of its activities and its social effect. The historian of the Cooneyites is faced with a formidable task.[31]*

This study will examine the movement's theology and review this against Bebbington's four characteristics of evangelicalism – the Bible, the cross, conversion and activism - as the criterion and a comparison of the gospel preached and taught by the 2x2s.

---

29   *The Secret Sect* written by Doug and Helen Parker and in a letter dated 16th September 2011 they have given me permission to quote from the book.
30   Wilson uses the term Cooneyites to cover the early movement and the current 2x2s.
31   Parker, Doug and Helen, *The Secret Sect*, (Sydney: Macarthur Press (Books) Pty. Ltd., 1982), viii.

Secondary Sources

The secondary sources fall into two distinct categories: (1) the scholars and sources that are quoted to verify and validate the characteristics of evangelicalism, and (2) others that are quoted to simply illustrate a practice that in the past has been a hallmark amongst evangelicals. It is therefore important to explain that the sources chosen are those which can illuminate and give substance to the characteristics of evangelicalism within the context of this research.

It is important to understand that this is not a critique of evangelicalism but a brief résumé of the sources used as references throughout this research. Because the characteristics of classical evangelicalism are the criteria used to assess the theology of the 2x2 movement it is important to justify the main secondary sources used to support this thesis.

Bebbington's quadrilateral first appeared in 1989 and it would be difficult to find any writing of scholarly importance on evangelicalism published since then that does not make reference to these characteristics either explicitly or implicitly. There is little doubt that this research could have justifiably used as a benchmark to assess the orthodoxy of the 2x2 movement some of the early church creeds. The statements of faith contained in the 'Apostles' Creed' or the 'Nicene Creed' would have led to the same conclusion. The contents of both of these and other such creeds are affirmed by most Protestant and Catholic groupings. One can satisfactorily show that these creeds echo the characteristics of evangelicalism as understood and accepted by all of the Christian groups that lay claim to this label. At this point it is more important to identify the theologians, and not necessarily their works, whose views will be quoted throughout this research in support of this thesis. The reason for this is that the statement or quotation from the relevant theologian that is most appropriate may be found only in another author's work.

A clear and concise view of the characteristics of evangelicalism is outlined in what has become known as Bebbington's quadrilateral – the Bible, the cross, conversion and activism. In evangelical thought these are looked upon as representing classical evangelicalism and were first expressed in Bebbington's book, *Evangelicalism In Modern Britain,* a work described by John Stott as 'Bebbington's magisterial survey.'[32] Commenting on Bebbington's quadrilateral, Noll writes, 'David Bebbington has identified the key ingredients of evangelicalism.'[33] A noted scholar and historian, Bebbington's work, *Evangelicalism In Modern Britain* was published in 1989 and his four characteristics of evangelicalism quickly became the benchmark for many other works on the subject of evangelicalism.

It would be difficult to research a subject with the characteristics of evangelicalism as its theme without reference to three theologians who are widely recognised for their work in this field of research – John Stott, Jim Packer and Alister McGrath, all of whom are Anglicans.

A forerunner to Bebbington's quadrilateral was Packer's six characteristics published in 1975 and these he described 'as chief among the truths of which evangelicals are trustees.'[34] The six characteristics are:

1. The supremacy of Scripture as God-given instruction, a sufficient, self-interpreting guide in all matters of faith and action;

2. The majesty of Jesus Christ our sin-bearing divine Saviour and glorified King, by faith in whom we are justified;

3. The lordship of the Holy Spirit, giver of spiritual life by animating, assuring, empowering and transforming the saints;

4. The necessity of conversion, not as a stereotyped experience but as a regenerate condition, a state of faith in Christ evidenced by repentance and practical godliness;

5. The priority of evangelism in the church's agenda;

6. The fellowship of believers (the faith-full) as the essence of the church's life.[35]

32 Stott, John, *Evangelical Truth,* (Leicester: IVP, 2003), 27.
33 Noll, Mark A, *The Scandal of the Evangelical Mind,* (Leicester: IVP, 1994), 8.
34 Stott, *Evangelical Truth,* 26-27.
35 Packer, J. I, *The Evangelical Anglican Identity Problem: An Analysis,* (Oxford: Latimer House, 1978), 15-23.

Commenting on Packer, McGrath writes, 'he is regularly cited by evangelical leaders and thinkers as one of the most important influences on their lives.'[36] McGrath adopted and expounded these six principles in his book *Evangelicalism and the Future of Christianity* published in 1994. McGrath had reduced these to four (broadly corresponding with Bebbington) in his book *A Passion for Truth: The Intellectual Coherence of Evangelicalism*, published in 1996. Derek Tidball is another theologian who has written widely on the subject of evangelicalism and in his book *Who are the Evangelicals?*, he posits that Bebbington's quadrilateral 'has quickly established itself as near a consensus as we might ever expect to reach.'[37]

Another scholar/historian who addresses the intricacies of evangelicalism is Mark Noll who is joint editor along with David Bebbington of *The History of Evangelicalism* series published by Inter-Varsity Press which includes Noll's book, *The Rise of Evangelicalism* published in 2004. Another book by Noll is *The Scandal of the Evangelical Mind* published in 1996.

It is the works of these theologians and their quotations that will be mainly used throughout this research to support the statements made throughout this thesis. The selection of these scholars is based mainly on the fact that they all endorse Bebbington's quadrilateral albeit that there may be minor variations in the order or interpretation. The importance of the views of Stott, Packer and McGrath in any work on evangelicalism is best expressed in the title of Roger Steer's book, *Guarding the Holy Fire – the Evangelicalism of John R. W. Stott, J. I. Packer and Alister McGrath.*[38] Commenting on Stott's relevance to evangelicalism, Tidball writes, 'one name that occurs more frequently than most in the text and the bibliography, that of John Stott. John Stott has made an enormous contribution to evangelicalism since the Second World War, serving as its foremost national advocate, leading international statesman and its chief apologist.'[39] In the foreword to Tidball's book

---

[36] McGrath, Alister, *To Know and to Serve God*, (London: Hodder and Stoughton, 1977), xi.

[37] Tidball, Derek J, *Who are the Evangelicals?*, (London: Marshall Pickering, 1994), 14.

[38] Steer, Roger, *Guarding the Holy Fire – the Evangelicalism of John R. W. Stott, J. I. Packer and Alister McGrath*, (Grand Rapids: Baker Books, 1999)

[39] Tidball, *Who are the Evangelicals?*, 3.

Noll also pays tribute to Stott when he writes, 'Tidball follows the best authorities: Scripture first, then the noble worthies of tradition like Edwards and Wesley, and finally the sanest evangelical voices today, especially, John Stott.'[40]

Most of these theologians are Anglicans who along with other scholars noted here are all unambiguously evangelical; their intellectual approach to the subject is objective, balanced and always anchored in Scripture. Their views will be quoted to support the various aspects of characteristics of evangelicalism, as will other scholars in support of biblical interpretation. Theologians and their works on biblical interpretation include Gerald Bray, D. A. Carson, James Dunn and Craig Blomberg. Craig Blomberg, distinguished professor of New Testament at Denver Seminary, was in Dublin in January 2012; I had the opportunity to discuss with him the Scriptures relied on by the 2x2 movement and his responses are in this thesis.

Bray is a scholar in historical theology and his works on creeds, councils and biblical interpretation support the basis for the use of Bebbington's quadrilateral. His writings help illuminate the importance of the atonement and the Trinity in the church throughout the ages. The works of Dunn give a clear insight into biblical interpretation and quotations from his works help clarify and support the findings of this research. Dunn's research has produced insights into the practices of the early New Testament church and helps illuminate these for the twenty-first century church. Quotations from his works have been used to either support or explain findings of this research.

Any work that seeks to establish an authentic account of how the first-century church operated within its cultural context simply must take into account the writings of Kenneth Bailey. An author and lecturer in Middle Eastern New Testament studies, Bailey has spent forty years in Egypt, Lebanon, Jerusalem and Cyprus. Therefore, his views serve to interpret New Testament Scriptures within their cultural and historical contexts.

----

[40] Tidball, *Evangelicals?* xii.

It would be difficult to study any research of importance without finding input from these theologians that is used to either validate or explain a point more clearly. These are not theologians and scholars who have been randomly chosen without strict regard to their suitability for use in this research.

Definitions

A major restriction in this research is the widespread nature of this movement in many countries over the world. They have adherents as far afield as the West Indies and Haiti. They have substantial numbers in the United States and Canada with smaller numbers in Australia and New Zealand. Nevertheless, on a per capita basis Ireland has more adherents to the movement than any other country. This of course is a natural progression given that Ireland was where the movement started and many of the adherents are fourth and fifth generation. Because of this, most of the sermons and testimonies will be mainly from Ireland. The study will utilise other sources of information where this is relevant and appropriate.

There are those who have entered into email correspondence with me. These are mainly members of the movement, some are workers and at least one is an overseer. They have requested anonymity and confidentiality of the source so it is important to respect this at all times. So that this correspondence is verifiable, details of emails and private messages are available to the internal and external examiners as they appear in the footnotes.

The conclusion as to how to define this movement will be based on their theology, beliefs, practices, and then to decipher, within the framework of Bebbington's quadrilateral whether they are evangelically Christian, an exclusive sect, a new religious movement or a cult. In the twenty-first century, there is such a plethora of religious movements that it is increasingly difficult to define them accurately. Bruce thinks:

> *A difficulty in talking sensibly about religious organizations is that we use the words like church, sect, denomination, and cult loosely and inconsistently. The prominent American archivist of new religious*

movements J. Gordon Melton, for example, follows journalistic
usage in describing any new religion as a 'cult'. As well as being
used promiscuously, such terms are also used to endorse or condemn.[41]

An important aspect of this research is the primary nature of the
material gathered through attendance at missions and conventions,
meetings with overseers, workers and members, past and present
together with the extensive email correspondence from various parts of
the world that helped present an authentic account of the movement.

In recent studies, the trend is towards the terminology of New Religious
Movements (NRMs) to define movements that are outside mainstream
Christianity. Any study of the complex phenomenon[42] of NRMs will
discover that a precise definition is difficult. Nevertheless, the term has
become the one chosen by many scholars in a conscious attempt to
eliminate the more sensational and pejorative connotations of other
terminology. The search is not only to describe a complex phenomenon
but also to use neutral language.[43] In general, NRMs is used to identify
religious groups that adhere to a theological perspective and a structure
or pattern of religious behaviour that is self-consciously distinct from
the dominant society and its mainstream religion. According to Saliba,
'three major, distinct (though sometimes related) definitions of a
cult emerge from a survey of current writings on the subject. These
definitions can be respectively classified as theological, (or religious),
physiological and sociological.[44]

According to Fox, 'the label is generally used by scholars in Europe
and America to designate religious groups that have either arrived in

[41] Bruce, Steve, *Religion in the Modern World*, (Oxford: Oxford University Press, 1996), 70.

[42] Chryssides, George D, *Exploring New Religions*, (London, Continuum, 2001), ix, comments
on this in the introduction to his book: 'Not only is the subject matter complex, but NRMs
are volatile, and it is likely that, even before this book reaches the public, affairs will have
moved on. I can therefore do no more than offer a snapshot of NRMs as I have found
them at the turn of the millennium.'

[43] Turner, H. W, 'New Mission Task: Worldwide and Waiting' in *Missiology*, Vol. XXXII
(1), 1985, 5-21, 20, writes of 'the age-old tension that arises when established and properly
conservative religions are faced by new, strange, innovative, unorthodox or wildly heretical
or outlandish religious movements'. Dispassionate (theological) approaches are possible, and
Saliba, John, *Perspectives on New Religious Movements*, (London: Chapman, 1995).examines
NRMs from sociological, psychological, legal and theological perspectives.

[44] Saliba, John, A, *Perspectives on New Religious Movements*, (London: Chapman, 1995) , 2.

the West after 1950 or are new to Westerners.'[45] In his examination of NRMs, Saliba goes back to the second century and starts with Gnosticism.[46] It is important to be aware of the large volume of scholarly writings and definitions of NRMs, but that is a separate study and not within the parameters of this research. I agree with Fox's observations:

> *More recently, scholars have also noted that the phrase "new religious movements" has begun to accumulate many of the negative connotations previously ascribed to "cults". Opponents of the phrase have charged that academics introduced it in order to deflect what they consider legitimate criticisms about the movement. In the face of such considerations, one suggestion has been that scholars of religion abandon the label and return to using the technical term of "sect" and "cult", having first agreed on their definition.*[47]

According to Chryssides 'there is no consistent, agreed sociological definition of "sect" and "cult".'[48] I would submit that this is one of the reasons why academics have gravitated to the use of NRMs as an all-encompassing umbrella. Within the field of theological research NRMs undoubtedly has a place but not necessarily to supersede the use of 'sect' and 'cult'.

Because this research will define the movement within the framework of Bebbington's quadrilateral of evangelicalism the point made by Chryssides is important: 'If Jesus Christ offers the sole means of salvation as evangelical Christians believe, then it clearly is important to ascertain whether any of the new religions can serve as a vehicle to mediate the divine grace to make available the effects of Christ's redeeming work.'[49] Sects are more difficult to categorize and according to Chryssides, 'tend to be small, unlike the established religion which dominates the culture and constitutes the religion of the majority.'[50]

---

45 Fox, Judith, 'New Religious Movements' in Hinnells, John, editor, *The Routledge companion to the study of religion*, (Abingdon: Routledge, 2005), 324.
46 Saliba, *Perspective on New Religious Movements*, 52.
47 Fox, Judith, New Religious Movements in Hinnells, John, editor, *The Routledge companion to the study of religion*, (Abingdon: Routledge, 2005), 326.
48 Chryssides, *Exploring New Religions*, 7.
49 Chryssides, *Exploring New Religions*, 24-25.
50 Chryssides, *Exploring New Religions*, 5.

Nevertheless, whilst many sects are heretical this is not the case for some sects who will affirm the doctrines of the Apostles' Creed but they may simply be exclusive in the membership requirements. Chryssides writes, 'in most sects, neophytes enter by means of a conscious decision, often publicly professed, in which they affirm their commitment to the sect's aims and values.'[51]

In contrast, cults are always heretical in nature in that they either deny the cardinal doctrines of the Bible or will add to these in such a way as to make them erroneous. For a theological definition of a cult Enroth states: 'A cult of Christianity is a group of people, which claiming to be Christian, embraces a particular doctrinal system taught by an individual leader, group of leaders, or organization, which (system) denies (explicitly or implicitly) one or more of the central doctrines of the Christian faith as taught in the sixty-six books of the Bible.'[52]

Failure of the 2x2 movement to exhibit the characteristics of evangelicalism does not mean that this is enough to label them a New Religious Movement, a sect or a cult. However, if it becomes clear throughout the research that the movement falls within the definitions[53] of a cult of Christianity then there will be no alternative but to state this as the conclusion. It is within the framework of these various definitions that this research will reach its conclusion on the 2x2 movement.

[51]   Chryssides, *Exploring New Religions*, 5.
[52]   Mather, George A, Nichols, Larry A, and Schmidt, Alvin J, editors, *Encylopedic Dictionary of Cults, Sects and World Religions*, (Grand Rapids: Zondervan, 1993), 381.
[53]   See other definitions on page 160.

Literature Review

There are a small number of books available on the movement and these have been generally critical of their doctrines and practices. Most conclude that they are a cult or at best an extremely exclusive sect. The writers or editors of these books are mainly ex-members.

Academically, the book that is of greatest value is *The Secret Sect*[54] written by Doug and Helen Parker and published in 1982. It is a detailed account of the movement from its beginnings and throughout most of the twentieth century. Parker's parents joined the movement in New South Wales when Doug was a boy. He was an Anglican minister in Australia where he now lives in retirement. With the foreword from the distinguished theologian, Professor J I Packer and the preface by sociologist Bryan Wilson, the book is widely accepted as an authentic account of the movement's history and beliefs. In the foreword, Packer writes:

> *A good deal of published material exists on most sects, but the community known as the Cooneyites, Go-preachers or simply Nameless Ones, though widespread, has not so far received scholarly description and evaluation in print. The Parkers' pioneer work, however, now supplies this lack. Based on personal experience in the movement together with careful research, and alert to historical, theological and sociological issues alike, it is a valuable contribution to knowledge and could be a godsend to anyone facing the claims of the sect and needing to assess them.*[55]

Wilson comments:

> *However, a "secret evangelistic organization" would appear to present a logical contradiction. Yet this description aptly fits the Cooneyites. So "secret" are they that they are no more than a name to most Christians, and even to most students of sectarianism. Theological students of comparative symbolics have discovered no more about*

---

54   Parker, *Secret Sect,*(Sydney: Macarthur Press (Books) Pty. Ltd., 1982).
55   Parker, *Secret Sect*, vi.

them than have the sociologists of religion.[56]

Following its publication, *The Secret Sect* received a blaze of publicity especially in the United States. In the early days, reports of 2x2 conventions appeared in some Irish newspapers. Occasionally in the United States a curious local reporter would venture onto a convention ground and write a short article but up until the publication of *The Secret Sect*, little was in the public domain. Publication of the book was a revelation to many outside Ireland of the real history of the group. Newspaper reporters in the United States who previously had largely ignored the 2x2s published details of the book.[57] The book is well researched and provides a very credible account of the history and practices of the movement. The book gives a detailed history of the origins of the movement that includes biographical details of Irvine, Cooney and some of the early workers. These are authenticated by personal interviews conducted with those who were around from the early days.

In November 1954, an interview with Irvine Weir, one of the team of early workers that started in 1899, reveals Cooney's first involvement with Irvine. Writing on this interview and on Cooney's personal testimony the Parkers comment:

> *Great sacrifices were made by many of the people who became preachers. Edward Cooney, the son of an Enniskillen draper, was first invited to preach at one of Irvine's meetings in Bonnosokane, [Borrisokane], County Tipperary. As he became acquainted with the new teaching he formed the opinion that "Irvine was a prophet raised up by God to lead back those into Christendom to the truth as it is in Jesus", and offered to back his mission but Irvine replied, God doesn't want your money. He wants you Edward. Convinced that was his calling, Cooney gave up his business interests in 1901,*

---

56   Parker, *Secret Sect*, vii.
57   These extracts and responses published, as in appendix 2, page 163 appeared in various US newspapers and are by no means extraneous since they show the confusion that exists within the movement in various places and the lack of a coherent understanding of its origins.

donated thirteen hundred pounds[58] and devoted himself to preaching.[59]

The book presents a picture of Irvine as a man who manifested various contradictions in his preaching and practices.[60] The Parkers explain that 'in 1901, Irvine resigned officially from the Faith Mission, George Walker and Matthew Wilson [fellow workers in the new movement] witnessed his formal resignation.'[61] The Parkers report:

> *Irvine and several of his companions prepared for a bicycle preaching tour of Scotland in the autumn of 1899. While there was no doubt on the part of the team members that the mission to Scotland was independent of the Faith Mission, when travelling there Irvine's mission team accepted the hospitality of Faith Mission supporters, as they did in Ireland, and were successful in winning some.[62]*

These actions of Irvine and the team portray Irvine and his team of workers in a light that the movement would like to erase. The book outlines the beliefs espoused by the movement and the major biblical doctrines they reject. It is wide ranging in its coverage of the movement and presents the information in a fair and objective way. Some of the information will be used in this study to support various arguments and conclusions posited in this thesis.

The Life and Ministry of Edward Cooney[63] written by Patricia Roberts[64] who knew Edward Cooney personally over many years provides an accurate insight into the man. The book is a hagiography in that it casts Cooney in the best possible light without any critical assessment. The book is an important contribution to the history of the movement and includes many details that would have been available only to the author and to those who were particularly close to Cooney. The

---

58 In today's value this equates to £117,533. Source: http://www.thisismoney.co.uk/money/bills/article-1633409/Historic-inflation-calculator-value-money-changed-1900.html. Accessed 28 September 2011.
59 Parker, *Secret Sect*, 6-7.
60 This will be addressed in more detail on the section on William Irvine.
61 Parker, *Secret Sect*, 6.
62 Parker, *Secret Sect*, 6.
63 Roberts, Patricia, *The Life and Ministry of Edward Cooney*, (Enniskillen: William Trimble Ltd), 1990.
64 Patricia Roberts met with me in her home on two occasions. October 2008 and 19 September 2011.

author confirms the major role that Cooney played in the early days of the movement although current 2x2s would like to rewrite this part of their history minus Cooney. Roberts would have a better insight than most into the situation that existed at the time of Cooney's excommunication because of the close family ties between, the Reid, West and Roberts' families. The excommunication of Cooney led to a family schism with the West and Roberts families supporting Cooney while the Reid family were strongly opposed to Cooney. This book is helpful in establishing early chronological developments.

The Church Without A Name by David Stone[65] gives a detailed view of the history and theology of the movement from one who spent time on the inside. This detailed work gives a critical assessment of their *modus operandi*. The analysis of the 2x2 terminology is most informative and helps the reader understand many of the nuances that are peculiar to the movement.

In the chapter on 'Understanding the Scriptures' the writer comments:

> *The workers willingly answer any questions from unprofessing people who are attending gospel meetings, but after anyone professes for several years, the ministry becomes less interested in answering probing about doctrine and even becomes defensive and threatened by innocent questions.*[66]

This is something that has been the experience of many former members. When one professes, they must not question but willingly accept what the workers say. Stone writes from the perspective of one who spent many years in the movement; 'I was an obedient member of this church for over forty years. Our family left voluntarily when we became aware that the doctrine was unscriptural.'[67] The book is a comprehensive survey of the movement and produces clear evidence as to why the writer concludes that their beliefs and practices are unscriptural. The author consented to the use of her material in this research.[68]

[65]   David Stone is the pen name used by Kathy Lewis
[66]   Stone, David, *Church Without a Name*, 157.
[67]   Stone, David, *Church Without a Name*, 43.
[68]   Email Kathy Lewis, 28th December 2011.

Kevin Daniel is the author of *Reinventing the Truth*. In a personal email Daniel writes, 'I've never been a member or attended 2x2 meetings, but have also had many and excellent opportunities to observe the recruitment and retention processes first hand.'[69] This book is a critical analysis of their history and exposes the steps they have taken, especially outside of Ireland and the United Kingdom to conceal their origins. He explains how the 2x2s have created a pseudo- historical account that deliberately misleads. One of the tracts he analyses was written by Dr Cornelius J. Jaenen who had a distinguished career as a chronicler of Canadian history and is a respected member of the Faculty of the University of Ottawa. According to Daniel, 'Jaenen is, or has been until recently, a member of long standing in the so called Two-by-Two religious group.'[70] Jaenen's tract, "The Nature of the First Century Church", according to Daniel, 'purports to shed some light on the characteristics, structure and early history of the Church under the original apostles . . . there are many disputable points raised in this.'[71] Daniel does a detailed analysis of this work and highlights errors that are presented by Jaenen[72] in such a way as to support the *raison d'être* for the 2x2 ministry.

A writer who grew up in the movement is Lloyd Fortt. Fortt has written *A Search for "the Truth"*.[73] Born in 1947 Fortt includes his personal testimony that covers his years as a 2x2 member and how the discovery of Parkers' *The Secret Sect* led him to ask questions and to leave the movement. He helpfully presents his book by alphabetically listing 2x2 terminology and theological words with an explanation of the 2x2 interpretation of these. This book supports the explanations by liberally quoting workers' utterances, some of which date back to the very early days of the movement.

---

[69] Email from Kevin Daniel, 12th January 2011.
[70] Daniel, *Reinventing the Truth*, 23.
[71] Daniel, *Reinventing the Truth*, 24.
[72] Jaenen has communicated with me by email saying that his views have changed since his early work. 'The excerpts in Daniel's book are unfortunately not what I believe - this was excerpted from a talk (probably to IVCF) at United College in Winnipeg many years ago when I started examining the possibility of an unbroken line of "workers." I found out that did not exist in fact.' Email, 13th December 2011.
[73] Fortt, Lloyd, *A Search for "the Truth"*, (Oregon: Research and Information Services), 1994.

The Church With No Name[74] was written by Lynn Cooper, a psychologist, born and living in New Zealand. Cooper was born into a 2x2 family and her grandparents joined the movement in the nineteen-twenties. She 'professed' when she was fifteen years old and spent fifteen years as an active member. This is a clear, concise and incisive work. It gives an accurate history of the movement and an insightful chapter on the question, 'why do people stay?'

An important book for reference is *The Apostles' Doctrine and Fellowship*, a documentary history of the early church and restorationist movements by Cornelius J. Jaenen. Following a comprehensive survey of the early church and movements throughout history there is a final section on Select Restorationist Movements. In the section Contemporary [Irish] Restorationist Movements, he writes:

> *By the last decade of the nineteenth century, a number of religious activities in the British Isles gave rise to a movement which first manifested itself at Nenagh, in county Tipperary, and soon spread throughout Ireland, and eventually throughout the world by the end of the twentieth century. This nameless spiritual fellowship, sometimes condescendingly referred to as the Two-by-Twos, espousing the ideals of apostolic preaching and evangelical poverty, participatory worship in the homes of the laity, and observances of the ordinances of immersion baptism and frequent communion, did not fit the sociological models of sect, cult or denomination. Although denounced in some religious circles as a secretive organization, it held public evangelistic meetings, welcomed investigation of its teachings, and became well known to many governmental authorities throughout the world.*[75]

This statement stands in opposition to Jaenen's remarks in his introduction when he writes, 'this documentary history should not be interpreted as an apology for primitive Christianity and of historical attempts to restore the primitive model.'[76] In section A, Jaenen comments on the New Testament church starting with the Gospels.

---

[74] Cooper, Lynn, *The Church With No Name*, published in 1996 and available online: http://www.thelyingtruth.info/?f=noname&id=2.

[75] Jaenen, Cornelius J, *The Apostles' Doctrine and Fellowship*, (Ottawa: Legas, 2003), 518.

[76] Jaenen, *Apostles' Doctrine*, 32.

The emphasis on the sending out of the apostles in twos in Matthew 10 and the sending of the seventy in Luke 10 sets the scene for the support of the 2x2 model of ministry. For anyone familiar with the 2x2 slant on the interpretation of the importance of the 2x2 ministry there is certainly a bias in favour of the 2x2 teaching. There is the emphasis on the church in the home to the exclusion of any other places where the early believers met and again this is an important tenet in 2x2 teaching.

In conclusion, Jaenen makes a very important observation and concedes, 'in our efforts to trace continuity of primitive Christian ideals over the centuries, no unbroken successions or continuous activities of a particular group have been documented. Nevertheless, no century appears to have been without some witness to those ideals.'[77] This conclusion is unwelcome news for many 2x2s who have in the past used Jaenen as an apologist for the idea of continuity of the 2x2s with the New Testament church.

There are other books on the 2x2s and these are useful in helping to create an authentic account of the movement's history, sociology and theology. Two excellent books published by Research and Information Services are *Reflections* edited by Daurelle Chapman and *Reflected Truth* compiled by Joan Daniel. These books are collections of the personal testimonies by former members, signed and validated, some of whom are former workers. Generally, they give a very clear and concise account of time spent in the 2x2 movement and the reasons that led to them leaving or in some cases being excommunicated. Some of those who have had their accounts published in these books have corresponded with me during this research, including Joan Daniel who compiled *Reflected Truth*. These accounts and testimonies have one common thread and that is that they had a false impression of what the 2x2s teach and believe simply because of what they were told by workers and others in the movement. When they asked questions as to the doctrine and practices they were viewed as troublemakers. Extracts from some of these accounts will appear as appropriate throughout this study.

Two other accounts are worthy of consideration and while neither

[77]   Jaenen, *Apostles' Doctrine*, 535.

is an academic work, they are nevertheless invaluable in providing details of the early days. Alfred Trotter's account of the movement in the early days is one that would never see the light of day if the 2x2s could suppress it. I spent a good deal of time trying to unearth this document, its existence was denied by those who should have known better. Trotter was born in 1894, wrote his account in 1968 and updated it in 1975. It consists of 193 hand written pages; it is clear and gives details that hitherto have remained in the background. There is nothing of a sensitive nature nor is there anything that would be damaging to the movement so it is difficult to understand the secrecy. We learn that Trotter's father was 'saved' during a mission on his farm in Glencar, County Leitrim in 1904 conducted by Jonathan Smith and John Hume. His father died prematurely in 1908 and in 1912 Trotter 'professed' at a mission in Enniskillen conducted by Edward Cooney. One of the most important features of this document is the gracious comments made about those who did not see eye to eye with the movement.

The other document is the account of Goodhand Pattison entitled simply *Beginnings* and written in 1925 at Cloughjordan[78] the place from where William Irvine launched the new work. The eighteen tightly typed A4 pages chronicle the movement and give a detailed account of it. Pattison's two sons became workers. His daughter had three sons [Donaldson] who also became workers. Commenting on Pattison's account, Trotter writes, 'The old man died about 1931 his wife having predeceased and he left behind the best and fullest account of the people of God.'[79]

There are other books, which are of less significance to this study, but which may be quoted from time to time.

---

[78] Cloughjordan is a small town in County Tipperary, Ireland and in 1925 had a population of 800 people.
[79] Trotter's account.

Origins and History

Despite the lack of written accounts of their history, it is possible to construct an accurate historical picture of the origins of the 2x2 movement and its subsequent development. In 1897 a Scottish Faith Mission pilgrim, William Irvine, proclaimed that he had a revelation that the only basis for the Christian ministry was in Matthew 10: 5-15. In 1901, Edward Cooney who became co-leader joined him. A growing number of men and women abandoned all of their possessions and joined the movement as preachers in the years between 1897 and 1905. The founder William Irvine was certainly enigmatic and is difficult to define. Pattison relates an account of a meeting in his home between Irvine and Cooney and although he does not date the event he says it was about one year after Irvine arrived. Immediately prior to this he refers to the Borrisokane mission. Roberts places the mission in 1897.[80] That would date the meeting somewhere in 1898. After the family had gone to bed, according to Pattison:

> *The two discussed so fully the subject of preachers and preaching of Matt. 10 sort, William pointing out the need etc. in the face of the greatness of the harvest and the fewness of the labourers and Eddie seeking to escape the issue one way or another. . . So about 2 o'clock in the morning he had won and Eddie decided to give up his bags and job and go forth with the result of becoming what you know him now.*[81]

Irvine continued to work with the Faith Mission and at the same time set up an independent mission until he resigned from the Faith Mission in 1901, the year Cooney became a preacher.

I have access to some very good primary sources from my mother aged eighty-eight years and other elderly relatives and friends. For example I know that in 1935 two 2x2 female workers, Jenny Wilcox and Gladys Cockburn, held a mission in the barn on my grandfather's farm in Lettermoney, Ballinamallard, County Fermanagh. At that mission my

---

[80]   Roberts, *Cooney*, 10.
[81]   Pattison, Goodhand, May 1925, 9, written three years before Cooney's excommunication.

maternal grandparents professed. It is my mother's recollection that the workers contacted her parents at the request of her mother's sister, Emma, whose surname was Creagmile, of a strong Methodist family in County Tyrone; she had emigrated to the United States and met with the 2x2s there. The 1911 Irish census shows that Emma, also known as Emily, was the youngest of the nine Creagmile children.[82] Sending news to workers back home may have been a trend at that time because another document[83] tells that two young girls emigrated from Ross Shire, Scotland, to New Zealand in the 1920s. They came under the influence of 2x2s and sent a request to the workers in Scotland so that they would contact their family and this led to this family also 'professing'.

Commenting on this phenomenon, Stone, author of *The Church without a Name* writes:

> *Cherie Kropp has done extensive background checking on the workers who came to the US and Canada and she has found that nearly all of them contacted family members from Ireland and Scotland. And this is the way that the group primarily grew originally was simply through family (sic). And it seems that it is primarily through family and friends and marriage that the group has managed to survive. The strength is more in family than in the workers' preaching or their theology. The people don't usually understand the workers' basic teaching, they simply believe what they have been told by people they trust. This is why it has been so difficult to biblically reason with them.*[84]

Although this movement had its beginnings in County Tipperary, it quickly took hold in County Fermanagh, the birthplace of Edward Cooney. Cooney was a charismatic figure and was a gifted orator, especially in open-air preaching which was very common at the beginning of the 20th century.

---

[82]   http://www.census.nationalarchives.ie/pages/1911/Tyrone/Tullyclunagh/ Aghnamoe/870687/.
[83]   Helen's account, 11th March 2009.
[84]   Email Kathy Lewis 10th May 2009.

The doctrine established by Irvine and Cooney was never written down except in sermon notes taken by members and reporters who attended their meetings. Irvine used certain verses to support his theology but ignored the rest of scripture that refuted his premises. Because Irvine never did publish his theology, Bible students have not been able to effectively point out its errors.[85]

A series of articles in the *Impartial Reporter* in June/July 2008 featured some of the early members of the movement in Fermanagh. An interview carried out with Mrs Ruby Ferguson, who turned 90 in October 2008, gives a useful and accurate insight into those early days. My mother agreed that the article was an accurate reflection of life in the movement in the early 20th century and for some there has been little change since then.

Ruby was one of five daughters of William and Harriet West of Mullaghmeen House. They had one brother, Harry, who represented Fermanagh and South Tyrone as a Unionist Member of Parliament in the nineteen-sixties and early seventies and was at one time Minister of Agriculture in the Stormont government of Northern Ireland. Her father, William, and his brother John were already believers and active in the work of the Methodist church and were early converts to the 2x2 movement. According to Mrs Ferguson, 'when they heard Edward Cooney preach on the Diamond in Enniskillen they were so impressed by his conviction that all organized religions had strayed from the humble example and message of Jesus Christ that they forsook their Methodist church to follow him.'[86] This seems to imply that they followed Cooney.

The week following the interview with Ruby Ferguson the *Impartial Reporter* featured Ruby's cousin, Dr Patricia Roberts whose parents also had been involved in the movement from the early days. Roberts is the author of a book on Edward Cooney and a number of other books that help build a clear picture of the movement's *modus operandi*, especially in the early days.

In my meetings with Roberts, we discussed early aspects of the

[85]   Stone, *Church Without a Name*, 37.
[86]   *Impartial Reporter*, 26th June 2008.

movement from both a historical and a theological basis. Roberts is one of a small number of those who remained loyal to Edward Cooney following his excommunication in 1928.

In her words, she 'was born again' through the ministry of Edward Cooney and personally baptized by him at Rossahilly, on the shores of Lough Erne, County Fermanagh. Roberts is well acquainted with the activities of the movement and the disputes that took place, and one of the major advantages of her information is that some of it she personally witnessed and the remainder was given first hand by Cooney and a large number of early adherents, many of whom were her family members.

From the beginning, the movement refused to take a name but despite their strong objection to taking a name, they soon had to forgo their principles:

> *1914 was a watershed for the movement. In order to be recognised as conscientious objectors during the First World War, they became a registered sect under the name of "Testimony of Jesus". This was a bitter pill for those who had rejoiced in being "the Sect with No Name". From being the only true followers of the first-century Christians, it seemed as they were now to be counted as just one more religious denomination.* [87]

They followed a similar registration process in other countries and often this name registration was withheld from the members. Their ministers have officially registered the group with various government agencies under the names of "the Christian Conventions" in the USA; "the United Christian Conventions of Australia"; "The Testimony of Jesus" in the United Kingdom and "The United Christian Conventions of New Zealand" in New Zealand.

In 1903 the 'Living Witness Doctrine' was introduced and this was to become the first major area of dissention and schism. Roberts describes the emergence of the doctrine: 'at first this doctrine claimed that one could be born again only through Irvine or one in the

---

[87]   *Ballinamallard a place of Importance*, (Ballinamallard Historical Society, no publication date), 71.

fellowship with him. But by 1907 this had been reduced to Irvine and his fellow preachers only.[88] Parker comments, 'because acceptance of the "Living Witness Doctrine" was made binding upon them by Irvine and the senior workers, some workers who regarded it as heresy were perplexed.'[89] This doctrine is still very strong amongst the overseers and workers and those who reject do so at the peril of excommunication. It is important to profile the activities of both Irvine and Cooney since both are generally viewed as the co-leaders albeit that Irvine was considered the prime mover. After he became a worker in 1901 Cooney quickly emerged as a co-leader alongside William Irvine. One newspaper reports, 'At last Sunday evening's service there were five men and two women on the platform, and of the former were two of the chief pioneers of the movement—Mr. Wm. Irwin[90] and Mr. Edward Cooney.'[91] Although the movement was started by Irvine, Cooney's contribution will be assessed first for two reasons. Firstly, Cooney had a much longer tenure in the movement than Irvine. Secondly, the current 2x2s believe and practice much of what were Irvine's teachings so this creates continuity between the assessment of Irvine and the critique of the movement's history.

[88] Roberts, *Cooney*, 57.
[89] Parker, *Secret Sect*, 19.
[90] This is obviously a misspelling of Irvine and occurs in many newspaper reports.
[91] *Impartial Reporter*, 18th July 1907.

Edward Cooney

Born in Enniskillen in 1867, the son of a wealthy businessman, Cooney was converted as a teenager in Armagh and immediately started to witness to his faith. Cooney was a charismatic leader and a passionate preacher and this led to him being ranked a co-founder of the movement from its early beginnings. Cooney was as forthright as Irvine in his condemnation of churches and clergy and was a driving force in the new movement and particularly so in his home county of Fermanagh. Cooney was an activist and he tirelessly preached whenever an opportunity arose, whether in a hall or open air on a market day. He preached regularly on the Diamond[92] in Enniskillen and Trotter records, 'So much has been written about Edward Cooney, the man through whom I professed myself. Cooney spoke in the open air and he could be heard nearly a mile away. He preached very effectively in Fermanagh and London and during his later years travelled to most English speaking countries.'[93] Despite his antagonism towards the clergy, even those with whom he did not agree judge him kindly.

Cooney was completely committed to the principles he believed were in Matthew 10 and these were apparently obvious in his lifestyle as a newspaper reports:

> *No one can say that Mr Cooney says one thing and practises another. Nay, the very thing which gives most force to his preaching is the fact that he himself practised the self-denial and abandonment of the world, which he preaches; that he gave up good commercial prospects to follow the Lord, and that in daily life he shares with his brethren in common, and gives of what he does not possess to those in more need than himself.*[94]

One Ballinamallard resident commented on Cooney's life of faith, 'I recall Cooney coming to the Ballinamallard train station, penniless, believing the Lord would supply a ticket for the journey and he was

---

92   The Diamond is in Enniskillen town centre, County Fermanagh.
93   Trotter account of the 2x2 movement.
94   *Impartial Reporter*, 13th October 1904.

never disappointed.'[95] Cooney's unwavering adherence to his principles and his abandonment of the 'Living Witness Doctrine' led to conflict with his fellow workers and his excommunication in 1928.

Commenting on Cooney in 1920 a fellow worker said, 'Edward Cooney was a very loving, kindly, special man. Even unprofessing people were impressed by him.'[96] Fortt writes, 'he was a dynamic speaker who was widely known in Ireland and Scotland in the late nineteenth and early twentieth century.'[97] There is no doubt that it was this strength of personality and his vitriolic condemnation of existing church models that led to the growth of the movement in the early part of the twentieth century. On Cooney's preaching at a convention, the *Impartial Reporter* reports:

> *In the unwarrantable attacks upon church organisations in general, and upon ministers of the gospel in particular, he makes a hobby of our Lord's forbidding the Apostles to provide either gold or silver or brass in their purses. The passage that contains the prohibition is he contends the permanent commission for all preachers.*[98]

The same newspaper records Cooney's testimony of his call to join Irvine's new movement. A report in 1904 from the *Impartial Reporter* indicates that it is evident that Cooney is emphasising the Matthew 10 model of his ministry:

> *"Three years ago," said Cooney, "the Lord said to me, Go, Edward Cooney, without scrip, and go into all nations, baptising them in the name of the Father, Son, and Holy Ghost, and teach them to observe, "all things whatsoever I have commanded you." Then he gave me His promise, "Lo, I am with you until the end of the world," and he has kept it.*[99]

---

95 Discussion with Ballinamallard resident, 15th February 2012.
96 Stone, *Church without A Name*, 161.
97 Fortt, *Search for 'the Truth'*, 290.
98 *Impartial Reporter*, 2nd June 1904.
99 *Impartial Reporter*, 9th June 1904.

Cooney's meteoric rise to co-leadership ended in 1928 when he was summoned to a meeting of senior workers convened in the home of Andrew Knox, Clankilvoragh, Lurgan, Northern Ireland. Along with other practices and teachings of the movement Cooney was in disagreement with the 'Living Witness Doctrine.'[100] This was not the only grievance that Cooney had with the direction that the movement was taking. He expressed his reservations on the organizational element that dictated where workers should serve.

> *In the late 1920's Edward Cooney began to denounce the "Overseers" for their arrogation of authority, the accumulation of money and worldly goods, their abandonment of the simple lifestyle originally proclaimed by the group, and their adherence to the "Living Witness Doctrine".[101]*

The Lurgan meeting consisted of twelve of Cooney's fellow senior workers and they requested Cooney submit to their authority. Roberts describes the purpose of the meeting as, 'this meeting was to make one final attempt to organize Cooney by binding him to decrees which he said would have restricted his service and suppressed the influence and power of God in his ministry.'[102] Cooney refused to agree to the conditions required, as did another worker at the meeting, Tom Elliot, and both were summarily excommunicated.

Substantial numbers within the movement remained loyal to Cooney, especially many in his home county of Fermanagh. These are now a dwindling number with no full-time workers and a few small cells in Northern Ireland, Australia and New Zealand. Those who remained loyal to Cooney and those who are known as the 2x2s initially differed little in behavioural patterns. Apart from the Cooney faction refusing to accept the 'Living Witness Doctrine' there seems little else that separates them. What is immediately apparent is that those who claim the Cooney heritage are more accepting of other believers and much less legalistic in their overall lifestyle.

There were many who felt that the overseers had acted in an autocratic

----

[100]   Roberts, *Cooney*, 57.
[101]   Daniel, *Reinventing the Truth*, 175.
[102]   Roberts, *Cooney*, 143.

way and ordinary members had no opportunity to either hear the case against Cooney or make their own judgement. Wilson Reid made it clear that the break with Cooney was complete in a pastoral letter to the members in Ireland in December 1928. Reid wrote:

> *We must make it known that we cannot ask Eddie or his companion to take part in any meetings we are responsible for, nor encourage any saint or worker to attend theirs. We feel we must henceforth advise them to stay away. We can't accept any responsibility for those who decide to go with Eddie nor those who profess in his meetings now that he is out of fellowship and on his own.*[103]

Reid joined the movement following a mission in 1903 on the family farm in Carnteel, County Tyrone and went into the work in 1904. In 1905 he went to South Africa as a missionary. Trotter writes, 'he returned to Ireland in 1913 and did a great deal of work mostly in the North until he returned to Africa in 1930.'[104] During this period, both Irvine and Cooney were excommunicated and afterwards the movement was referred to as Reidites. One strong voice in support of Cooney was that of James Bothwell, their bishop in Irvinestown, County Fermanagh. He was responsible for the organisation of special meetings. Roberts records his efforts:

> *Despite the crisis in the fellowship, the Christmas meetings were held in the Orange Hall in Irvinestown as planned. James Bothwell, the bishop of this community, as was his custom made all the necessary arrangements. Wilson Reid, the chief worker in Ireland, was to preside over the meeting.*[105]

Reid failed to appear, Bothwell asked Edward Cooney to preside, and a number of people left the hall but the majority stayed to hear Edward preach. A letter from Bothwell to Reid regarding his absence from the meeting indicates that feelings were strong:

> *I was rather surprised when you turned away, as I did not expect you to do such a thing. You said you were sorry for those who would be*

---

[103]   Parker, *Secret Sect*, 76.
[104]   Trotter's account.
[105]   Roberts, *Cooney*, 150.

> *disappointed thereby. I would remind you that a true shepherd would
> not flee when he would see the wolf coming, as I take it you don't
> think Eddie is a true shepherd. Then you should, if you were a true
> shepherd have taken care of the sheep.*[106]

The letter then refers to a meeting in his home when Hugh Breen, a
senior worker, presented their case against Cooney.

> *I did all I could to have all present, thinking there might be something
> wrong with Eddie, but when all was told, I found nothing to condemn
> Eddie for, no evidence, but only untrue reports written by jealous
> or false brethren carried across to this country. Now this is what
> I thought of the meeting held here first. And another thing which I
> think was unkind, was to come round behind Eddie's back and pour
> in all the poison, and him not there to defend himself.*[107]

The division was bitter and even penetrated into family relationships.
According to Roberts, this split had a divisive effect not only on the
movement but on her entire family circle.[108] The strength of feelings
aroused by the division is clear in a letter written by William West to
George Walker, an overseer in October 1929:

> *You said when you were here that it would be no harm for anybody
> who felt so inclined to go and hear Eddie; and again at the Christmas
> meetings in Irvinestown I heard him explain the differences that
> had arisen between the brethren and himself. I went to see him at
> Rossahilly where he was staying. Now as a result of this, instead
> of being treated the way you said, the first thing I found was two
> workers (Sam McClements and Hugh Breen) going round the saints
> that came to the church in our home and warning them not to come
> any more. . . The charges that Wilson Reid brought against him,
> put on paper and circulated against his brother in Christ were so
> easily refuted, and of such trivial character that even Eddie's enemies
> admitted there was nothing in them. . . To come to the sad happenings
> in this county, immediately after Christmas last two workers spent
> almost all their time during the winter and the spring going around*

[106]   Roberts, *Cooney*, 150.
[107]   Roberts, *Cooney*, 146.
[108]   Discussion with Patricia Roberts, 19th September 2011.

> *the little churches and then around individuals, applying the test of whether or not people believed in Cooney. Churches were visited on Sunday mornings for the sole purpose of closing them, including the one in my home, Mullaghmeen. Several of them were actually closed. . . In my case, a new church was formed at Reids of Gortaloughan (my brother in law) and now half the church meet there. The other half continues to meet in my home.*[109]

Cooney continued his itinerant ministry and finally died in New Zealand in 1960. Following his excommunication a large number continued in fellowship with Cooney in Ireland and in other parts of the world. The opinion of one 2x2 with whom I met and is now an octogenarian who professed in his teens, is that the division was very badly handled and resulted in much hurt and dissention, especially in County Fermanagh where Cooney continued to have considerable support.[110] Regardless of denials by present day 2x2s of Cooney's important role in the formation of the movement, there is ample evidence that indicates that he was viewed a co-leader in the early days.

At my last meeting with Roberts,[111] I explained that my own recollection of Cooney, whom I had met a year or so before he died, was that he had a broad acceptance of believers from other Christian denominations, something that he spurned in his early ministry. Roberts pointed out that this is part of the reason why he was excommunicated. She qualified Cooney's position in that whilst he believed there were genuine believers in other denominations, the denominations themselves were wrong. His view stemmed from the fact that he always saw his own conversion as a young teenager in Armagh as the starting point of his Christian pilgrimage. The decision to excommunicate Cooney in no way dampened his enthusiasm for the model of ministry that he had pioneered and he continued until his death in 1960 as an itinerant preacher.

Cooney is difficult to assess in that some of the principles he espoused at the beginning of the movement he later rejected and these included

---

[109] Roberts, Patricia. *The Go Preacher Movement – An Anthology*, (Enniskillen: William Trimble, 2000), 57.

[110] Meeting on 20th January 2012.

[111] Meeting with Dr Roberts in her home on 19th September 2011

the divisive 'Living Witness Doctrine.' He was passionate and sincere in his belief that he professed faith in Christ as a young man in Armagh and was therefore more generous in his judgement of others than some of the workers who had known no other influence than the 2x2 movement. It is best to let an outsider who knew Cooney well assess his contribution. Few are better qualified to do this than the Fermanagh schoolteacher/evangelist and a highly regarded Methodist lay preacher, George Coalter, who writes:

> *Now I should like to add a complimentary word about Edward Cooney. He is now full of years like myself, and finishing the course. He has a wonderful personality and is gifted with a great intellect. I did not agree with his drastic statements but nevertheless I loved the man for his sincerity and for living a life of poverty when he could have been possessed with riches. We have no scales to weigh the value of tireless devotion to cause of righteousness and truth but he who holdeth the seven stars in his right hand, knows his works, tribulations and poverty and if faithful unto death he shall receive a crown of life.[112]*

[112]   Coalter, George J, *My Memoirs 1890 – 1950*, (Enniskillen: William Trimble, 1951), 55.

William Irvine

From Kilsyth in Scotland, William Irvine (born in 1863) was converted at Motherwell town hall following the ministry of a Presbyterian evangelist, Rev. John McNeill.[113] He started to prepare for Christian service by attending the John Anderson Bible College in Glasgow for a short time before joining the Faith Mission as a pilgrim on 14th June 1895 and as recorded in *Bright Words*[114] moved from his native Scotland to work in Ireland with the Faith Mission in 1896.[115]

Spirit of Revival is a history of the Faith Mission, an interdenominational evangelistic mission, written by I. R. Govan, a daughter of the founder, John George Govan. Born in Glasgow he came to a personal faith in Christ in the Island of Arran when twelve years old. Govan answered the call in 1885 to leave business and become a preacher beginning in the districts of Loch Lomond and Irvine. The following year he started the Faith Mission and this spread throughout the United Kingdom and Ireland. The work consisted of preachers, pairs of women and men holding evangelistic missions in existing churches or community halls but working closely with the churches within the community. Their preachers, known as pilgrims, by 1891 had commenced work in Ireland having started in Blackrock, County Dublin.[116]

John Long was Irvine's co-worker in the new movement. Long, a Methodist, worked as a colporteur for the Methodist Church. William Irvine publicly excommunicated him from the platform in the 1907 convention in Crocknacrieve because he refused to embrace the 'Living Witness Doctrine.' In the best traditions of Methodism Long kept a journal and this gives an account of his work between 1892 and 1927. On close examination of his journal it seems that it is the best insider eyewitness account we have of the early days in the movement. I have verified the authenticity of the journal with John Long's son, the Reverend John Long who has the original manuscript. Extracts

---

113   Parker, *The Secret Sect*, 1.
114   *Bright Words* is the official magazine for the Faith Mission.
115   *Bright Words*, 15th November 1895, 267.
116   Govan, I. R, *Spirit of Revival*, (Edinburgh: Faith Mission Publishing, 1938), 99-100.

from Long's journal appear in many publications and the full journal is published on the website. [117]

Reports in the *Bright Words* magazine[118] indicates that Irvine was an active and popular worker for the mission and started with promise.

> *'NENAGH — Eight months ago, before the advent of the Faith Mission, it would have been almost impossible to "unearth" more than a dozen live Christians in this town … When Pilgrim Irvine arrived here last August, he found the spiritual light of the place burning dimly. However, before he closed a six weeks' mission, several backsliders were restored, and a number of souls had yielded to the Holy Spirit's pleading, and are now rejoicing in the excellency of the knowledge of Christ Jesus'.*[119]

Irvine's dedication to the work of the Faith Mission was soon to change and from March 1900, *Bright Words* reports , 'Pilgrim Irvine is in the south of Ireland. We have not had regular reports from him lately.'[120] In *Bright Words* August 1901 Irvine's name has disappeared from the list of pilgrim workers. Govan makes a report of a visit to Ireland, 'a number of young people are going out on quite independent lines holding missions in various parts both of Ireland and Scotland. . . as some have been mistaken for pilgrims, we think it necessary to say that the Faith Mission is not responsible for this movement.'[121] This was an obvious reference to Irvine's new movement. Parker confirms, 'in 1901, Irvine officially resigned from the Faith Mission.'[122]

There continued to be some confusion regarding Irvine's status and his links to the Faith Mission and in May 1903, it was necessary for *Bright Words* to carry statements on two other occasions distancing Irvine and his workers from the Faith Mission. The statements appear in full in appendix 3.

---

[117] I wrote to John Long 31st January 2009 and visited him at his Ballymena home on 5th February 2009 when I viewed the manuscript. http://www.tellingthetruth.info/publications_johnlong/index.php.
[118] Full extracts are published in appendix 3, pages 165-167.
[119] *Bright Words*, 15th April 1898, 91-92.
[120] *Bright Words*, March 1900, 56-57.
[121] *Bright Words*, August 1901, 175-176.
[122] Parker, *Secret Sect*, 6.

Irvine's behaviour from 1897 until his resignation from the Faith Mission in 1901 raises many important ethical questions. Daniel writes, 'In 1897, he [Irvine] began preaching independently, although he was still being subsidized by the Faith Mission as head of its missions in Southern Ireland. Several of Irvine's converts and associates from the Faith Mission attached themselves to Irvine's movement at this time.'[123]

Despite Irvine's revelation in 1897 that the church should be based on the idea of Matthew 10, which was that of unsalaried minister, there is ample evidence from Long's journal and other sources that Irvine remained as a paid preacher with the Faith Mission until his resignation in 1901. In view of his early convictions that all other church models were in error it seems odd that he should continue his Faith Mission ministry, which entailed working closely with the established Protestant denominations. Two possibilities for the delay in making a clean break exist. Did Irvine wait until such times that he had built up a healthy numerical following or did he resign when he realised that the Faith Mission was unlikely to tolerate his double life style for much longer? 'For several years Irvine accepted the hospitality and support of Faith Mission members while he propagated his own ideas.'[124]

Despite his convictions that Matthew 10 was the model for Christian ministry it appears that he was content to remain a paid preacher of the Faith Mission while building up support for his independent ministry. If the founder of the movement lacked openness and transparency then it did not bode well for its future. When we find 2x2 workers lying about the origins of the movement and denying the existence of men such as Edward Cooney, we can see a parallel with Irvine's stance. Stone provides us with an excellent illustration of the double standards that exist:

> *Kathleen Holland, a sister worker for over fifty years had a conversation with a professing couple in California. She related several personal accounts of Eddie Cooney, revealing that she knew him personally. She finished the conversation by saying, "Now, if anyone ever asks you about Eddie, you tell them NO SUCH A PERSON EVER EXISTED!"*[125]

[123] Daniel, *Reinventing the Truth*, 169.
[124] Parker, *Secret Sect*, 3.
[125] Stone, *Church Without a Name*, 161.

Stone comments, 'the friends and workers don't even blink about such lies. They have no conscience about anything they say regarding the church for they believe evasion of truth is justified in such instances.'[126]

Irvine's new movement quickly established the two distinctives that remain to this day. These are those of the church in the home and homeless preachers. The idea regarding homeless preachers is based on their interpretation of Matthew 10:5-15. The movement expanded quickly, initially throughout Ireland. The lists show four full time workers in 1901 and this had expanded to fifty-five by 1905.[127] Many of the early workers left Ireland to establish the movement in the United States, Canada, New Zealand, Australia and South Africa. Long's journal makes an entry following their first convention in Rathmolyon, County Meath, in 1903 that confirms their early missionary activity. It was from that conference that a few workers including William Irvine, went to America for a gospel tour.[128]

Both Irvine and Cooney had a strong antipathy to existing churches and many of their sermons included bitter attacks on the clergy and other denominations as the following report shows:

> *The meeting opened with the singing of hymns and prayer. The most interesting address was that of Mr. Wm. Irwin, (sic) who dealt solely with the clergy and the terrors of hell. . . . Mr. Irwin (sic) is a forcible speaker, and has a very convincing manner. He spoke of the clergy of all denominations in scathing terms and stated that in all ages the clergy were the marks of the devil. Jesus, he said, would never have a clergyman, and his own personal belief was that every clergyman would go to hell unless he turned and worked in what he called 'the Jesus way.' He also added—'No one in heaven believes in the clergy, and no one in hell either.' His idea of hell is rather novel. He described it thus:—'Hell is a place where every man will be made to serve God in the Jesus way.'[129]*

---

[126] Stone, *Church Without a Name*, 161.
[127] Stone, *Church Without a Name*, unnumbered page in the book's appendix.
[128] *Long's Journal.*
[129] *Impartial Reporter*, 18th July 1907.

The first major convention was in the home of John West,[130] Crocknacrieve, County Fermanagh, Ireland[131] in 1904. Thereafter, an annual convention has become an event in the 2x2 calendar in every country where they established a work.

Held in high esteem by the workers Irvine's word was law. 'Their respect for him as the voice of God to them in their youth went on by easy and imperceptible stages from respect to love; from love to unbounded admiration; and from admiration to idolatry.'[132] A change of wind was evident in 1909 and there was developing an attitude of antipathy towards Irvine and his leadership but his star did not wane overnight. 'Apparently those who knew him well noticed a change in Irvine's manner at the Crocknacrieve convention in 1909 when he was absent from most if not all of the public meetings.'[133] Despite the power and authority wielded by Irvine, his days were seemingly numbered and he was excommunicated in 1914. Those responsible were some of his early converts who then usurped the power base. As we examine the changes in Irvine's views from the inception of the movement there seems little doubt that he was the architect of his own downfall. Parker explains:

> *Although Irvine complained about the failure of some preachers to keep Matthew ten, and even though some preachers who knew him well were uneasy about his more indulgent life, genuine disagreement arose between them and Irvine when he turned to second adventist teaching. . . Irvine believed He [Christ] would anoint the two witnesses, John and himself, to have power over drought and plagues.*[134]

The new content of this preaching caused major concern amongst the workers and according to Parker, 'sectarians were perplexed at the oddness of his preaching.'[135] They baulked at the esoteric nature of this new revelation and were not prepared to accept it. Parker writes, 'Irvine followed the tendency among sectarian founders to seek for

[130] John West was a brother of Patricia Roberts' mother.
[131] Ireland was one country in 1904. Partition did not come until 1922.
[132] Letter from Alfred Magowan to Edward Cooney cited in *The Secret Sect*, 18.
[133] Parker, *Secret Sect*, 61.
[134] Parker, *Secret Sect*, 62.
[135] Parker, *Secret Sect*, 62.

himself a Biblical identification which he found in the martyred figure of the second witness of the book of Revelation, chapter eleven.'[136]

Parker confirms that the move against Irvine came with the approval of the leading workers:

> *Jack Carroll expressed his view that Irvine was no longer worthy of their loyalty, and would not accept anyone else's help or advice, Edward Cooney agreed with him that William "had lost the Lord's anointing".[137] One of the early converts, William Carroll, then overseer in Victoria, Australia informed Irvine of their decision to take control in April 1914. No public announcement of his rejection was made at conventions and his position was left open to surmise, so the reporter who visited convention meetings in Ireland in 1914 was able to write only of him that he stayed in Co Meath and that his health was not as good as usual.[138]*

Irvine's charisma and passion played a vital role in starting what today would be termed a New Religious Movement and he was able to gain a substantial following in a relatively short time. According to Fox, 'New religious movements are usually led by charismatic leaders whose teachings are often at odds with established religious practices and cultural norms.'[139]

But all was not well as Parker writes, 'although he was idolised by many in the sect, and many were devoted to his teaching amongst the workers his hot temper was feared, and his continual criticism revealed the existence of a conflict that he could not resolve successfully.'[140] Following his exit from the movement, Irvine moved to live in Jerusalem from where he remained in contact with some of the early adherents of the movement. He died there in 1948. Prior to his conversion Irvine was a Freemason. One correspondent writes, 'I encourage you to tell them that William Irvine was a Mason for over 50 years and that his belief system is modelled after Masonry.....not the Bible. . . the letter

[136] Parker, *Secret Sect*, 63.
[137] Parker, *Secret Sect*, 63.
[138] Parker, *Secret Sect*, 64.
[139] Fox, 'New Religious Movements', 335.
[140] Parker, *Secret Sect*, 62.

from the Grand Lodge of Ancient and Free and Accepted Masons of Scotland [which] says that he was a lifetime member. He was initiated in January 1884 and raised to the Master Mason Degree on January 17, 1885.'[141] This may be an explanation as to why many of the 2x2 missions are in Masonic halls.

When Irvine was expelled in 1914 and a similar fate followed for Cooney in 1928, the movement was free of their two founding fathers and could build itself along the lines it continues to follow up to the present time. Unlike Cooney, when Irvine was removed from power he did not have followers who joined him and he was left practically isolated.

The movement was noted for its missionary zeal in the early days and after its formation workers travelled overseas to spread their version of 'the truth'. According to Parker, 'in the year of 1903, William Irvine and Irvine Weir began preaching on the streets of Massachusetts. . . William Irvine travelled to Australia in 1905-6 where he was impressed favourably with the pioneering work achieved by John Hardie in New South Wales.'[142] An update of the fruits of those early missionaries was given at two Irish conventions in 2010. Speaking at the Fermanagh convention, Andy Robijn, a South African worker referred to those early workers who brought the message to South Africa:

> *In the country of South Africa where I come from, the first workers that came to our land came from here, came from the British Isles. In 1905 there were sixteen workers that left the British Isles on a ship. . . its destination was Australia and New Zealand. . . It stopped off at the port of Cape Town and it also stopped at place called Port Elizabeth, 600 miles around the tip of Africa from Cape Town, and it stopped again at the Port of Durban, another 400 miles up the coast. . . And today in our country there are twelve conventions and we have a staff of 36 active brothers and 42 active sisters, and our staff covers 8 countries in Southern Africa an area almost the size of Europe.[143]*

---

[141] Email 28th December 2011. I have a copy of this letter sent to Cherie Kropp from the Grand Lodge of Antient Free and Accepted Masons of Scotland, 10th December 2010. Masonic halls in Ireland and in other countries are frequently used for 2x2 missions.
142 Parker, *Secret Sect*, 32-33.
[143] Fermanagh Convention, Sunday morning, June 2010.

Speaking at the Cork Convention, a West Indies national worker, Rosalyn Warner, commented, 'When I came to these lands I couldn't help but think that the first workers that left these lands on a ship to go to the West Indies with the gospel (sic). The first ones left in 1924, and Jamaica was the first Island they stopped at. They got to the Island of Barbados in 1928.'[144] Workers still go overseas to preach but when it comes to providing other aid to people where poverty and hunger are rife, they do not get involved.

History Critique

The history of the 2x2 movement is complex in that no official records exist. The two most authentic accounts come from the hands of Alfred Trotter and Goodhand Pattison. Both of these men were close to the source and although both were part of the movement, their accounts are very honest and generally fair. Cooney's contribution has already been analysed so this critique will consider Irvine's role and the overall history.

The introduction of the 'Living Witness Doctrine' in 1903 was divisive and led to the first cracks in the fledgeling movement. This doctrine taught that one could only come to faith by hearing the gospel message from a worker. This doctrine was embraced by Irvine and most of the other workers and of course this bestowed upon them a power and authority beyond what they would otherwise have. Many of the men who accepted this doctrine had already professed faith in Christ before coming into contact with the movement. Both Irvine and Cooney professed under the ministry of others many years earlier and according to the Trotter and Pattison accounts, confirm that many who joined the ranks of the movement in the early days were already believers. Some of the well-known names of the early movement, John Long, George Walker, John West, Tom Betty whose wife Elizabeth had previously been a Faith Mission pilgrim were all believers prior to its formation. The 'Living Witness Doctrine' is still alive and well in the

---

[144] Cork Convention 2010.

minds of the majority of the movement who continue to believe that unless the gospel is heard from a worker one simply cannot become a believer.

Given Irvine's interpretation of Matthew 10 as the model of ministry as instituted by Jesus for all and meaning that all preachers would work in pairs in an unsalaried, home ministry, it is clear that in 1898 he was preparing for the new movement. While dining with the Reverend J. O. Park, a Methodist minister, and Cooney, Irvine proclaimed, 'there is no good clergymen, it's a contradiction in terms.'[145] According to Pattison it was 'Irvine who "proclaimed from the housetop" that all and sundry of the cloth [clergymen] including Mr Wesley [John] are in hell.'[146] There is a tone of disapproval when Pattison recalls, 'Mr Park is the man through whom I had professed conversion during his ministry in Dunmanway'[147]

While holding these views on clergymen and churches Irvine continued to associate with them, using their churches for missions under the auspices of the Faith Mission. It is undisputable that during his tenure with the Faith Mission he received his income on a regular basis but in the background he was busy laying the foundation for his new movement. Records reveal that the first workers in the new movement started in 1899 and that Irvine did not resign from the Faith Mission until 1901. Photographic evidence shows Irvine participating in a mission to Scotland in 1899 with some of his new workers.[148] Following his resignation from the Faith Mission and despite his aversion to clergymen this did not prevent him from having the Reverend George Grubb, a regular speaker at the Faith Mission and Keswick conventions, preach at one of his missions in their newly erected portable hall in Nenagh. The only reason for using Grubb in this mission would be to attract those in the area who were Faith Mission supporters and induce them to leave their churches and join the new movement. That may seem cynical, but given Irvine's antipathy to the clergy, it would be difficult to find another motive. Another anomaly is that in 1903

---

[145] Pattison, 17.
[146] Pattison, 17.
[147] Pattison, 17.
[148] Parker, *Secret Sect*, 5.

Irvine obtained permission to hold a two-week mission in a Methodist Church in Brooklyn, New York. It is fair to posit that if the Methodist leaders in that church had known of Irvine's blanket condemnation of all clergy and churches such permission would not have been forthcoming. Taken as a whole, regardless of his zeal and fervour, it would be difficult to come to any other conclusion than that Irvine was a man without integrity. With so many lapses into unethical behaviour, it would be difficult to give Irvine the benefit of doubt and describe him as inconsistent. To describe such behaviour as rank hypocrisy may seem strong but it would be difficult to put any other construction upon it.

If the founder of the movement found it easy to act in a way that lacked integrity and was essentially dishonest this is hardly a sound basis for the road forward. There are numerous accounts of some of the early workers leaving Ireland to work in other lands without being truthful as to the movement's origins. Irvine's demise from the movement that he founded came in 1914 when 'it became clear that William Irvine had a weakness for women, and other leaders of the movement insisted that he step down from leadership if he were to remain in the fellowship. He refused – and withdrew from them.'[149] His exit was not in a blaze of glory.

The movement was launched by men who claimed a revelation as to the way that Jesus Christ would want his church structured and the message based on Matthew 10 was plain, simple and plausible. This had an appeal, especially in country areas where people were more accustomed to small mission halls and Faith Mission style ministry that supplemented the work of the churches. In a paper, 'Ireland: religion & culture 1870-1914', (Department of History, University College Cork), Myrtle Hill writes, 'the Ireland of the late nineteenth and early twentieth centuries was a country where the largest majority had church connections. While telling us little about the practice of faith, census statistics [1901] allow us to outline the religious make-up of Ireland's population in the post-Famine era.'[150] The breakdown of

---

149 *Ballinamallard- A Place of* Importance, 71.
150 http://multitext.ucc.ie/d/Ireland_religion__culture_1870-1914. Accessed 21st February 2012.

religious groupings in Ireland in 1901 is interesting especially within the context of this study. Hill writes:

> *A little over three-quarters (76.9%) of the Irish population belonged to the Catholic Church, 12.34% were Anglican, and 9.2% were Presbyterian. The most important of the minority religions were Methodists at 8%, and 'others'—Baptists, Brethren, Quakers, etc.— together amounted to less than 1%. By the time of the First World War in 1914,[151] there had been a slight decrease in the number of Catholics (73.86%), and slight increases in Anglicans (13.13%) and Presbyterians (10.04%). There were also important changes in other congregation sizes: Methodists by 1914 made up 1.42% of the population, and others accounted for 1.55%.[152]*

Various reports of the early days of the 2x2 movement indicate that the Methodist church was the one that lost most members to the movement.[153] Hill's paper indicates that Methodists made up 8% of the Irish population in 1901 and by 1914, this had fallen to 1.42%. In the same period, there was a reduction in the Catholic population but small increases in the Anglicans [Church of Ireland] and the Presbyterians and only an increase of 0.55% in other denominations. The 2x2 movement would have been in its embryonic stages in 1901 but certainly had major growth in the years up to 1914. However, it would be difficult to deduce from Hill's research that the reduction in the Methodist population in Ireland was because large numbers defected to the 2x2s. The increase of 0.55% in other denominations does not necessarily reflect the growth of the 2x2 movement since many of them refused to state their religious affiliation on the census. One significant feature is that despite the simplicity of their model the movement had no success in attracting Roman Catholics who formed a large proportion of the population. From the early days there was

---

[151] There are two Irish censuses, 1901 and 1911. Therefore, whatever source used here in 1914 may not be strictly comparable with the 1901 official census.

[152] http://multitext.ucc.ie/d/Ireland_religion__culture_1870-1914. Accessed 21st February 2012. On the Irish census many in the new movement simply answered the religion question, 'information refused' and it is not possible to ascertain the actual number

[153] Trotter account, 'In those early days the Methodists furnished most of those who were willing to work in the way of God. And two prominent Methodists of those days were John West and Tom Betty who were intimate with one another'.

a tendency to hold missions in Orange halls (and there still is) so this would have alienated the Catholic population.

The numbers would have peaked during the first twenty years or so and one elderly 2x2 commented, 'there could have been as many as twenty thousand in Ireland alone but it is hard to put an exact figure on it.'[154] With around 4000 in Ireland now,[155] this represents 0.1% of the population and the numbers continue to contract. According to one source, a 2x2 who has lived in a number of countries and now lives in England, 'numbers in the United Kingdom continue to fall and numbers in North America, Australia and New Zealand have fallen over the past twenty years but now remain stable. It is difficult to quantify other countries.'[156]

Workers were certainly much more proactive in their outreach work during the early years of the movement. Trotter recalls:

> *She told us of some men who had called at her house looking for a place to have a gospel meeting. These men had come on bicycles having cycled I believe from Enniskillen and made a tour of the area. . . Tom Betty was one of the great stalwarts of County Fermanagh; a county which he helped open up and it now has more saints to the square mile than then possibly any other place in the world. He worked successfully in the various parts of Ireland and moved to the Isle of Man where after many years of good work he died in 1939.*[157]

These workers cycled the countryside, visited homes inviting people in the area to their mission that was usually held in a large barn on a local farm. Their presence was evident in open air preaching in town centres, especially on market days. It is easy to understand why men and women who showed such passion and enthusiasm as they extolled the virtues of a ministry along the lines of Matthew 10 and at the same time showing how far the churches were removed from this concept, would have had a wide appeal to simple country folk. When cracks

[154] Discussion in Fermanagh on 19th January 2012.
[155] Confirmed by Tommie Gamble, email 13th February 2012.
[156] Telephone discussion following email 8th December 2012.
[157] Trotter account of the early days.

in the movement began to emerge first with the removal of Irvine in 1914, and then with the demise of Cooney in 1928, the halcyon days of expansion were at an end and some thoughtful members abandoned the movement. In the words of Hammond, 'it is only natural that those who committed themselves to a rash enterprise and afterwards regretted their action, should be disposed to question the absolute sincerity of those who invited them to make a rash venture.'[158]

---

[158] Hammond Statement. http://cat.library.moore.edu.au/uhtbin/cgisirsi.exe/x/0/0/57/5. This was a short statement prepared and printed for the New South Wales Council of Churches, 'Go Preachers and Cooneyites', in 1955 by Archdeacon T C Hammond. It was only available from the library in Moore College, Sydney and was scanned and emailed to me by Paul Williamson, 19th August 2011. The full statement appears in the appendix 5, page 170-171.

Sociological Aspects of The 2x2 Movement

To examine the history and the theology of the 2x2 movement and exclude examination of their sociology would leave an important gap in this study. The movement seeks to give the impression that they are without hierarchy or organisation and that their entire *modus operandi* is by the leading of the Holy Spirit. This study will show that this claim is unfounded. Commenting on the movement, Bruce writes, 'those groups which do not actively encourage organization have some. After all, the Cooneyites[159] do meet. They have enough in common to distinguish them from their neighbours, so though they may disclaim any label other than "Christian", they do recognise each other.'[160] One ex-member from the US wrote:

> Upon reflection, I would certainly agree that the dress code of those in the fellowship community of my youth (particularly for women - longer dresses, long hair, no make-up, etc.) could be considered the basis for a common identity at the time. . .   other factors may be involved in sustaining the identity of this group.
>
> As a child, we did not have a television nor a radio in the house. We did have a radio in the car. I did not go to movies nor school dances. These were all "behavioral" differences from my friends in school. I would say that as a consequence I felt that I was "different" from my friends. I understood that this difference was in spiritual beliefs. I recall being told by my mother that we were a "peculiar people". Hence these differences did lead to an awareness of "common identity" with others in the fellowship.[161]

In Ireland, most members appear to know each other. To maintain purity within the movement they inter-marry. Consequently, many 2x2s are related through marriage and many marry 2x2s from other countries. For example, many Irish 2x2 marry someone from the US or another European country.

---

[159]   The name used by Bruce for the 2x2 movement.
[160]   Steve Bruce, *Religion in the Modern World*, 70.
[161]   Email 2nd October 2008.

The Structure

The structure within the movement is hierarchal although 2x2s seem to live in denial of this. They do not have a worldwide leader but a series of overseers (sometimes known as head workers). If a region is very large such as some of the States in the US there is a head overseer to whom other overseers report. The next level is the worker and these are ranked in terms of seniority of service but regardless of service, males always have precedence over females. Daniel confirms this, 'Female *"Workers"* do not rise to become *"Head Workers"* nor do they appear in other positions in which they outrank male *"Workers"*.'[162] Then there are the elders/bishops appointed by the workers to oversee each local fellowship. It is difficult to define this role but one thing that it is not is the teaching role for elders as in Titus 1:9.

According to Stone, 'ministers [workers] choose the elders and deacons who conduct the Sunday morning fellowship meetings and mid-week Bible studies, respectively.'[163] Elders are in subjection to the workers and Fortt writes, 'next there are male members who are in subjection to the local elder.'[164] Women members are in subjection to their husbands or other males. Fellowship and special meetings are for members only but the annual conventions are open to outsiders but rarely any attend. The meetings that the public are encouraged to attend are gospel missions and these are held during the winter months and usually on two or three nights each week. It is rare for outsiders to attend these in any significant numbers. Notifications of gospel meetings are by advertisements in the local press and a flyer put through the letterboxes of the local community. These are misleading since they state that these meetings are non-denominational. Since they are exclusively a 2x2 gospel meeting it is difficult to support the idea of 'non-denominational'. Attendance at all meetings by members is mandatory and failure to attend is closely monitored. Fortt confirms this when he writes, 'every "professing member" is expected to attend

---

[162] Daniel, *Reinventing the Truth*, 15.
[163] Stone, *The Church Without A Name*, 10.
[164] Fortt, *A Search for the "Truth"*, 97.

every meeting possible, and failure to do so without sufficient reason such as a serious illness, is seen as "back-sliding," and will invite a "little visit" by a *worker* and discipline if continued.'[165] There is no evidence of spontaneity in the gospel meetings or conventions. Meetings have the same format and there is never a variation. Even the times are rigidly adhered to. Hymn singing at 2x2 meetings is doleful and not like that of 1904 described by Trotter, 'the singing was hearty and would not pass muster with a music teacher. There was no musical instrument and the hymnbook was *Songs of Victory.*'[166]

'*HYMNS OLD AND NEW*' is the hymnbook of the 2x2 movement and the only publication they have, apart from the Bible. A number of hymns are written by their own workers and some are written by outsiders who are well known in Christian churches. This publication does not name the authors of the hymns or acknowledge copyright, which is a rather strange omission. Paradoxically some of the hymns are written by authors that the movement would describe as hirelings and false prophets. These include, 'Jesus the very thought of thee' by Bernard of Clairvaux and 'When I survey the wondrous cross' by Isaac Watts. Rather ominously they changed the words in Watt's second verse from, 'Save in the cross of Christ my God', to 'Save in the cross of Christ my Lord'. There are those who posit that this change reflects the movement's views on the deity of Christ. There are other hymns where there also have been word changes. Overseers and workers did not respond when asked about these.

---

[165]   Fortt, *A Search for the "Truth"*, 118.
[166]   Trotter account.

Conventions

The highlight of the year for the 2x2 members is the annual convention and all members are expected to attend their local one and some will attend several others as well. For example, in Ireland there are six locations. Attendance at these presents the observer with a meeting format that must be as far removed from the early church as it is possible to be, usually a large marquee with seating capacity of around one thousand, a platform situated centrally at the front and congregation around in a semi-circle. The workers sit on comfortable seats facing the platform on each side with male and female workers segregated. There is little or no evidence of an outsider having drifted in. In Ireland the convention speakers are usually local workers with a few visiting overseas workers. This was different in Sweden[167] where there are relatively few local workers and there were more overseas workers from the US, Canada, Scotland and Northern Ireland.

The 2x2 movement is a worldwide network and although they deny having a headquarters or formal organisation, they will quickly identify each other regardless of the part of the world they come from. An example of this was the Swedish convention of July 2011. Apart from the Swedes and a number of others from Scandinavia, there were attendees from Australia, New Zealand, Northern Ireland, Scotland and the United States and they all appeared to know each other very well. Every December they publish a list of the convention dates for the incoming year and the locations and dates remain fixed. Each country has a head worker and it would be his[168] task to pair workers for work in various parts of the territory. This will also include the organisation of the annual conventions and the allocation of workers to the various conventions. For example, the Irish list for 2011 shows the six conventions as Monaghan, Cork, Laois, Fermanagh, Down and Antrim. It then shows the worker in overall charge with the address of the convention grounds and telephone numbers.

---

[167] I attended the convention in Stockholm, Sweden for three days in July 2011.

[168] The use of the masculine gender is highly appropriate since there is no evidence of a head worker being anything other than male.

Ireland's six convention centres are used for only four days a year. A visitor to these grounds can clearly observe a campus complete with sleeping quarters, segregated for males and females, washrooms and toilet facilities both for those who stay on the grounds and for visitors. It must be emphasised that despite their protestations as to the lack of hierarchy, workers have separate accommodation. The conventions traditionally are on a farm belonging to one of the members[169] and preparations for the conventions start at least a month or so in advance. In Ireland as in other places, this will entail the preparation of the accommodation block, cooking facilities, dining area and the erection of a marquee, the preparation of sleeping and catering areas. The senior worker allocated as the worker in charge of the convention will direct all of the activities leading up to and during the convention.

For a movement that draws a veil of secrecy over its finances major questions remain unanswered as to the costs of hosting annual conventions and the maintenance of convention grounds. There is no doubt that there is a concern as to the true ownership and management of convention grounds. For example, in September 2011 the new convention ground in England was purchased in the name of a Northern Ireland company where the directors, a husband and wife, are members of the 2x2 movement. Convention grounds need renovation and maintenance to meet health and safety standards and to comply with fire prevention regulations and it is unlikely the owners can afford these costs since quite often they are in retirement. Admittedly, some of these venues are a going concern in farming and the Swedish venue is a successful market gardening venture. However, many of the buildings on these locations are not fit for anything except the provision of sleeping and eating quarters at convention times.

Considering the expense involved in maintaining these venues, it is somewhat disingenuous for the movement to point a finger at churches as though they are morally superior. Most denominations prepare a set of accounts every year that are transparent so that the membership and even those outside the membership know the income and outgoings. If we listen to the comments of ex-workers, there is a strong suspicion

---

[169] It is the same location each year.

57

that this movement has millions invested in various funds to which they have access but these remain secret from the membership at large.

An ex-worker who left to get married and was later excommunicated posted:[170]

> *In our day and age, and the standard required, it would be impossible to operate a convention of any size without access to these central funds - - much of the International travel and workers sent to other countries is also dependent on these funds put away for that purpose. Again, at this point I am not implying misuse of these funds -- Just that they are large, and that they do exist. The claim to organizational poverty is very clearly a fraud. The fraud is justified on the reasoning that it is "best for the kingdom"!!! (sic) Similarly to how they justify workers getting visas to hard to get into (sic) countries by deceitfully (to authorities) claiming they are students. Truth and integrity can be effectively negotiated around whichever way they choose within 2x2ism.[171]*

This is a serious indictment, and one that has not been contradicted by others, and points to a movement that not only works within a veil of secrecy but appears to think that the end justifies the means. Another ex-worker in the US posted:

> *The workers are not doing well to have the overseers in charge of the money. They are not being open about the finances. If they have nothing to hide, then don't hide it. Again, they are working on a technicality. "I don't have any money" while saying in their head ("because a trusted friend has all my money and gives it to me as I ask for it"). Just like they say, "I am not a minister" ("because I was not ordained on paper by an institution"). The workers are used to equivocating and bend the truth to fit them.[172]*

These are only two of the many comments that follow a similar line.

---

[170] The posts used from the TMB are only from those posters with whom I have verified through personal correspondence.
[171] http://professing.proboards.com/index.cgi?board=general&action=display&thread=18718&page=1. Accessed 14th February 2012.
[172] http://professing.proboards.com/index.cgi?board=general&action=display&thread=18718&page=1. Accessed 14th February 2012.

They point to a movement where there is a lack of probity in financial matters and this must erode the trust of those members who are deeply committed to the idea that this movement reflects all that is good in the New Testament Church.

It is recognised that there is considerable cost in running the conventions, especially when the travel costs of workers involve a considerable amount of international airfares. To justify the lack of transparency, the overseers will quote, 'let not thy left hand know what thy right hand doest' (Matthew 6:3). This is rather typical of how they will take Scripture out of context to justify an action. While the text calls for the utmost secrecy, it is within the context of giving to the needy.

Members

The qualification for membership of the movement is through 'professing' and while some would try to equate this with conversion in evangelical terms there is a difference. I have had several explanations as to what it means and will fully address this under the heading of conversion. Briefly, professing is a public indication at the end of a mission or sometimes convention that one now wants to follow Jesus and submit to the authority of the movement.

The constant picture that the movement presents is the uniformity of the movement throughout the world, but this is not the case. When it is pointed out that a particular practice is different elsewhere the response is, 'we are of the same spirit'. Some uniformity seems to remain in its patterns of behaviour on a worldwide scale with stories of similar experiences of those born into 2x2 families. The strong parallels that emerge especially among those in Ireland, the United Kingdom, Canada and the United States of America points to strong leadership despite the denial of a hierarchy within the movement. For example, the format of annual convention meetings is the same in Sweden as in Ireland and according to reports from workers, the same in every country.

Many former members of the 2x2s have outlined their experiences to me both during their time as members and how they have been treated since leaving or in some cases being excommunicated – a term not officially acknowledged within the movement. Rather surprisingly in a discussion with the Irish overseer he acknowledged that they do excommunicate but only for serious matters on which he did not elaborate.[173] Many of the 2x2s in the last few generations were born into the movement and their parents led them to believe what they were taught by workers, albeit without foundation. Because of this, many of the members live in a state of ignorant bliss as to its origins and beliefs. An Irish man, now in his mid-fifties, whom I have known for more than forty years writes:

> *I was born into a family in the North of Ireland where my mother and father were professing members of a sect, which is commonly known amongst people generally as "Dippers" or Cooneyites. I was taught at an early age that the fellowship did not have any official name or title since Jesus had never named his church and this was the "Only True Way" as it had never deviated from the Bible's teachings. We were always told that "The Truth" had never changed i.e. since the year 33 A.D. As a young boy I remember asking my mother what happened to the people like the native Americans, Aztecs, Aboriginal peoples who never had the opportunity to hear the "Truth" and her answer was that they would be cast out into outer darkness. Any argument that this was very unfair went on deaf ears – it was their tough luck. The only exception to this rule was the Jews, who although they denied the being of Jesus and all his teachings, (which to me was three or four steps down the ladder from the innocent bushman), were God's chosen People because it said so in the Bible; - I could never understand that logic. While the world around changed dramatically the one true way had continued unhindered for 2,000 years.[174]*

---

173 Discussion with Tommie Gamble 13th February 2012.
174 Email 11th March 2009.

The typical member in the movement is from a middle-class family and many are owners of successful businesses or farming enterprises. They live in districts that are middle class or better. One elderly 2x2 member who was born into the movement and professed as a young man confirmed this when he said:

> *They say things have not changed over the years but they have. A poor man no longer feels at home around the meetings, it is all about wealth, the best of cars and fine houses. It is changed days from the workers were happy to sleep in the back of their wooden halls. Now they will stay only in the best homes where they must have internet access and driving first class cars provided for them by the friends. Even the preaching has changed, it is more about the sacrifice of the workers than of the sacrifice of Christ.*[175]

A younger man who left ten years ago, pointed out that, 'the less well-off members feel out of place with all of the opulence that exists amongst the friends. The workers will only stay in the best of homes and the poorer families have got to do with the workers calling in for a cup of tea.'[176] In the early days, workers strongly advocated a life of poverty and frugality but this seems to have changed.

[175] Meeting with a 2x2 member, 26th January 2012.
[176] Discussion 16th February 2012.

61

Dating and Marriage

This is an area where there is little continuity in rules and regulations in the 2x2 movement and this seems to vary from country to country and even within the regions of the United Kingdom and Ireland. Members are forbidden to form a relationship with the opposite sex unless they too profess. Breaking this rule leads to disciplinary action by the workers. One man's story in this area is a typical reaction.

> *You did not date girls unless they were from within the fellowship, and eventually after finishing my education, I left home to escape my overbearing mother, and went to live and work at some distance from home and I made a new life in a new area. . . [I] eventually met the girl I was to fall in love with and marry. We had been dating a while and as a Methodist [she] was interested to learn about my religion. It so happened there was a mission started in our town that year and having been asked to bring any interested party to hear "the gospel" I duly brought my fiancée, even though I had not made her existence known to many of the "friends" as they like to call themselves. After attending 2 or 3 meetings, I was nabbed [taken aside] by a worker, Irvine Pearson one Sunday after the morning meeting and told in no uncertain terms that I was gravely transgressing by associating with a sinner, and I was no longer permitted to attend the morning meeting or partake of the emblems. I was shocked to my boots, since the worker also made many disparaging remarks about my family. . . I never darkened the door of any meeting house again.*[177]

One young 2x2 confirmed, 'this is happening today. It's just hidden but it is still happening.' [178] This is in keeping with a definition of marriage by Lloyd Fortt who describes marriage within the 2x2s as, 'an honourable decision which is given very little chance to take place, since dating is often viewed suspiciously as an "appearance of evil" (especially dating a non-member).'[179] Fortt sent me a personal email

---

[177] Discussion in Cork June 2010.
[178] Discussion 14th February 2012.
[179] Fortt, *Search for "the Truth"*, 117.

with his testimony that reflects this experience. He writes, 'there did not seem to be a way around this, and we were taught that dating outside of the sect was a no no. I found the girls at school much easier to get to know, but that "appearance of evil" stopped me from having a lot to do with them for a long time, and caused me to feel very guilty.'[180]

One 2x2 couple that I have known for more than forty years seemed to me to be rather ill matched. I mentioned this to one of their close relatives whom I know very well and the reply was, 'Oh, the workers got them together and arranged that marriage.'[181] Since members are restricted to marrying another member this limits the choice of life partner and Stone posits, 'there have been many cases of people marrying someone in the Way simply because there was no one else to choose from. They didn't (sic) love them at the time and hoped they would learn to love them. I have heard a few workers speak as if arranged marriages would be preferable.'[182] Workers officiate at funerals but they refuse to participate in weddings and therefore marriages take place in Civil Registry Offices. For those who claim that Jesus is their example and that they follow His ways this is an anomalous situation and contrasts with the record in John's Gospel (John 2:1-10), that the first miracle Jesus performed was when along with his mother and other disciples he attended a wedding and turned water into wine. Here we have Jesus in at a festive event enjoying food and drink in the company of his friends. Blomberg points out that, 'there are no references to notorious sinners present on this occasion, nor even those who are ritually impure.'[183] One of the first workers in Ireland who became a leading overseer in the United States, Jack Carroll gave very specific guidance to those getting married:

> For any to send a wide or general invitation to the Lord's people in any city or community, is entirely out of order. The parties getting married should remember that the friends to whom each invitation are sent, are only theirs as a result of the labor and sacrifice of others and that they never would have known them apart from the Gospel. .

---

[180]   Fortt, *Search for "the Truth"*, 307.
[181]   Discussion on 19th January 2012.
[182]   Stone, *Church without a Name*, 81.
[183]   Blomberg, *Contagious Holiness*, 123.

. There are just two places where we can encourage marriage of those "professing" to be the Lord's people to be held and two only - - the home or the office of the Justice of Peace or Judge.[184]

This statement of guidance is typical of the convoluted stance taken by the movement. There is no explanation of how their friends are only theirs 'as a result of labour and sacrifice of others' which is obviously a reference to the workers. Workers believe that their authority on matters of relationships, marriage and family is final. As one elder stated at a meeting, 'our workers are near the level of Jesus. Some are at His level. Jesus is very human and our example.'[185]

Confusion really reigns amongst the 2x2 overseers and workers when divorce is an issue. There seems to be no coherent policy in place to handle the complications that arise. One woman in Northern Ireland related her story:

> *I am sixty years old and was born into a 2x2 family and at age fourteen professed. I was deeply committed to the movement and adhered to what the workers requested, following all the rules, letting my hair stay long, wearing only skirts or dresses and certainly no television or radio. I married another 2x2 and moved to live with him in his native Scotland. He died prematurely leaving me with three small children. . .*
>
> *I met a man who also professed and was a divorcee. In 1988 we wanted to marry and this got the approval of Horace Todhunter, then 2x2 overseer in Scotland. Prior to the marriage we moved to Northern Ireland and then the difficulties started. The workers and elders in Northern Ireland forbade us to marry because my future husband was a divorcee albeit that he was fully accepted as part of the meetings. When we decided to proceed with our marriage we were excommunicated. The conditions attached to the excommunication was that we were not permitted to attend 2x2 conventions, special meetings, Sunday morning fellowship meetings or gospel missions. This was beyond what rejection usually is and is no further attendance*

[184] http://www.tellingthetruth.info/workers_articles/marriageb.php#February12. Accessed 7th February 2012.
[185] Fortt, *Search for "the Truth"*, 193.

at the fellowship meetings or special meetings. The workers were Sam Dewart, Bertie McKay and Tommie Gamble. There may have been others.

Both of us were heartbroken at this ruling and for the next three years made several efforts to gain repatriation but it all fell on deaf ears. By 1991 we gave up trying to gain readmission but we were traumatised and deeply hurt by the way which we treated and this included being ignored by friends whom I had known for a lifetime. This put a massive strain on our marriage since my husband had a strong yearning to be back in the meetings. In 2002 we separated and ironically my husband was readmitted to the fellowship. Since then we divorced and he is now living in England and a fully-fledged member of the fellowship.[186]

This woman attends another church and simply cannot understand why she was treated this way and why there was such a difference of opinion between the overseer in Scotland and the workers in Ireland. This illustrates the lack of consistency in the rules, depending upon the view of an overseer or worker in a region. But then such anomalies are not at all unusual as Daniel writes, 'remarriage to other than the original spouse following divorce is allowed in some parts of the Eastern U.S.A. and Canada, but results in exclusion on the continent [Europe].'[187] Situations like these demolish the myth that the organization enjoys worldwide continuity. Fortt highlights a situation that certainly finds no support in Scripture. He writes, 'if the unprofessing spouse holds strong beliefs at odds with two-by-two doctrine, attends a church elsewhere, or is otherwise deemed "an enemy of the Truth", the professing spouse may even be encouraged to divorce. In most areas, this is the only reason permitting a member to divorce while maintaining respectability within the group.'[188]

....

[186] I met with this woman on 17th January 2012 and she related her account at our meeting. To ensure accuracy I then emailed the account to the woman who confirmed it correct.

[187] Daniel, *Reinventing The Truth*, 17.

[188] Fortt, *Search for "the Truth"*, 54.

Sexual Morality

Over the past three and a half years between conventions and missions I have heard more than fifty sermons from workers from various parts of the world but mainly Ireland. The subject of sex was only briefly mentioned once and then it was tagged on to a few words at the end of a sermon where the speaker's message was mainly on Paul's writings to the Colossians, Timothy and Titus. Ireland's overseer, Tommie Gamble stated:

> *So these letters that Paul wrote, there's a lot of things in them and he said to these Colossians that they were to mortify their members which were upon the earth. And the first thing he mentioned about fornication, uncleanness, I don't want to go into those things, but he said, Paul said in one of these letters that fornication should not be at any time named amongst us. But in every letter he mentioned it, not to Titus or Timothy, but in all other letters he mentioned fornication. And I believe what he was meaning, that it shouldn't be mentioned. But in his day it seemed to be heavy placed. And he said I hear that there is fornication amongst you. It's a soul destroying thing, keep away from it. You young people make sure that you will remain a virgin, that's God's purpose for you. And you need to pray to keep pure and keep holy and God will help you. And the time is gone, we'll sing the grace.*[189]

Given the New Testament emphasis on the seriousness of sexual sin, 2x2 workers should give more prominence to this subject and give their members soundly based scriptural reasons to abstain from sexual sin. I discussed this with Gamble and explained that this was the first time I had heard a reference to the topic and he believes it needs to be addressed more often.[190] In discussion with one Irish ex 2x2 in his sixties he commented, 'of course we were all sexually active [males and females] in our teens and twenties and thought there was not much harm in it as long as we were not caught. Staying over at conventions

---

[189] Fermanagh Convention, June 2010, Sunday evening. Tommie Gamble was the closing speaker.
[190] Discussion with Tommie Gamble 13th February 2012.

provided new opportunities.'[191] Another former 2x2 who is a few years younger, was fully in agreement with this comment. Fortt writes, 'fooling around with the opposite sex outside wedlock, though not condoned, is somewhat less likely to receive much attention.'[192] Failure to address topics that are culturally relevant and where sound teaching is essential is a serious indictment of the workers' lack of responsibility. Stone comments, 'many girls during dating years, have mentioned that professing boys often attempt to take great liberties and show less respect towards them than unprofessing boys do. It is to be noticed that since girls are unable to use their attractiveness to win a husband some have resorted to sexuality to win one.'[193] A woman from Tasmania shared her story that sums up the outcome from the failure of sound teaching. She writes:

> *I was brought up with meetings in the country (SA) with meetings in our home every Wednesday night and I had a strict but quite a happy childhood. I married my ex-husband at 17 as I was pregnant (and very naive!) and was married for 13 years. He was abusive and mentally unstable and still is and he sexually and emotionally abused myself and our 3 children (2 girls and one boy) - he still is in the church (believe it!) and says he is never getting another partner as he doesn't believe in divorce whereas I have repartnered (sic) and have truly 'moved on'. There is so much that has happened that when I tell people my story they almost don't believe me - the unfortunate thing is I married a monster in a church which supports the perpetrators not the victims.[194]*

Although I have had a significant number of stories about the breakdown of marriages and the negative impact on family life, I would posit that it is more the exception than the rule. Since childhood I have known many happy and contented 2x2 families but this in no way minimizes the hurt felt by those who are badly let down and at times discriminated against by the system.

---

[191] Discussion in Fermanagh and Cork, June 2010.
[192] Fortt, *A Search for "the Truth"*, 79.
[193] Stone, *The Church Without A Name*, 64.
[194] Private message, 7th February 2012.

Funerals

Workers do officiate at funerals and, as well as friends and neighbours of the deceased, members are expected to attend even if they only vaguely know the deceased and the family. Sermons by workers will sometimes make little or no mention of the deceased. This may be different where workers have known the deceased well and stayed in their home. According to Stone, 'they are usually centered on the importance of getting right with God, which means of course professing.'[195] One example is of a funeral service where the link between the life of the deceased and the importance of the ministry was emphasised in the message by David Newlands who said:

> *I have faith in my heart today to believe there is one who made the law and made all things. The Gospel has confirmed that to me. To think about the Creator and not just creation. We are grateful today that obviously this was in the heart of our sister Edna, that day came in her life when she saw all this about her, the beauty of it all but she came to realise there was one behind the law, one behind the precept and one behind this beautiful order and it caused her to seek God and seek her Saviour. I am not going to say much about Edna because I don't think that Edna would want us to say anything. When we look at a beautiful statue, a lovely picture, we don't praise the work of art but we praise the one who made it. We saw the marks of salvation in her life and my companion [fellow-worker] and I who were homeless – I tell you, friends, and believe me when I say this today, there is no people on earth today like the homeless preachers of Jesus Christ who appreciate the kindness of those who open their home to us. No one like us who appreciate the spread table, the comfort that is there and the kindness when one is homeless. I say today, we appreciated the comfort of John and Edna's home. We praise the one who put that Spirit into her heart to open her life and her home.*[196]

---

[195] Stone, *Church Without A Name*, 77.
[196] Funeral service conducted in North of England by David Newlands and Evan McKay, 22nd May 1998.

Here we have the emphasis on homeless ministry and workers use every opportunity to get this concept over whether at a funeral or a mission meeting. An interesting development by the movement is when church buildings of other denominations are used by the 2x2s for funeral services. One report is, 'last week [1st November 2011] the funeral service for the overseer of BC Canada was held at the "Christian Life Assembly" church. Recently in Australia, the funeral of a 2x2 was held at a Presbyterian church. There must be a worldwide change of policy toward other Christian churches.'[197] This move represents a sea change since there was simply no way that a funeral service could be held in a church because churches are viewed as false. It is only in recent years that a 2x2 adherent will attend a funeral service of someone from another denomination. In the past sometimes they would attend but would not enter the church building.

Rules

A number of unwritten rules govern members and obedience to these rules is an important part of ensuring final salvation. Of course, overseers and workers deny that there are any rules but the evidence contradicts that. Although difficult to justify from a biblical perspective the rules are very much in evidence. This story will sound familiar to thousands of present and former 2x2s around the world, and many others who have contacted me echo similar stories. A forty-one year old South African woman who was born into a 2x2 family wrote to me as follows:

> *We were brought up to shun the "worldly" ways. I was not even permitted to join Girl Guides, let alone do ballet. Fortunately, making music was part of our family ritual and I enjoyed playing instruments. I was permitted to play classical music, excepting on the Sabbath and a Saturday night, when only hymns were permitted. What I found particularly damaging being brought up in this way was that, when I left home, I had no concept of what was wrong or right. It appeared that everything was wrong: dancing, TV, wearing*

---

[197] http://www.votisalive.com/content/paul-sharp-funeral-false-church-christian-life-assembly-circa-11-1-11. Accessed 22nd February 2012.

jeans or jewellery, make-up, movies, smoking, drinking, sport on a competitive level, cutting hair, manicuring nails - hell (excuse the pun), even a pretty engagement ring was frowned upon as unnecessary adornment.[198]

The claim that their standards have remained constant over the years starts to fall apart on scrutiny. For example, there is little in common with the 2x2s at the beginning of the twentieth century and those of the early years of the twenty-first century. Whether we read the experiences of those in Ireland, England, the United States, South Africa or New Zealand we find that although the workers claim that nothing has changed evidence points otherwise. Dress codes especially for women remain quite similar in that they are forbidden to cut their hair, they must not wear make-up or jewellery, they must wear skirts or dresses and plain shoes. Dress codes for men appear a little more relaxed although in many places facial hair does not meet with approval. Preaching at the Cork convention, Wilson Greene, a worker stated:

But anyway, as the conversation went, it went to this thing of boys with long hair down to their shoulders, it was in the films, the woman of that home said, long hair is not going to keep a boy out of heaven, so that is irrelevant. I was absolutely shocked. It did not take me long to come to the conclusion, I understand why your boy's outside the Kingdom. Now it's no need for me to go any further and try to help you for to understand the folly of that, but little things can grow and sometimes people will say, well that's immaterial, that irrelevant, and because of that well then something else's going to come. What is it doing? It is only following the patterns and passions of the world. Does the Bible not tell us long hair is a shame for the man, what more does a person want to know? I very nearly felt like saying to that woman, you need to read your Bible again.[199]

---

[198] Email 13th March 2009.
[199] Wilson Greene, Cork Convention, June 2010.

This statement indicates that Greene believes that the length of a young man's hair will keep him out of the kingdom of God. Of course, there are inconsistencies as one former member points out:

> *In the fall of 1966 I started college in eastern Iowa. It didn't take long to notice that "the way" in Iowa had some different practices from "the way" in Washington. Some women still wore black stockings and long dark skirts. There were no radios or other music components in home or cars and boys and girls didn't go swimming together. Why were these ultra conservative practices adhered to in the Midwest but not in the Northwest? I said little but my peace of mind was definitely disturbed.*[200]

In the sixties in Ireland radios and televisions were absolutely forbidden in a 2x2 home (they still are). I recall that when motor cars first came with a radio as standard equipment, members of the movement would certainly have removed both the radio and aerial. There is of course anecdotal evidence of Irish workers in that period breaking aerials off cars that did not conform! Radios are no longer removed from cars but whether they are used is a moot point!

One former member writes:

> *A young people's meeting that was held at Ron Good's home in the 1970s. At that meeting the young folks had gathered, there with the intent of discussing with the workers anything that bothered them. The meeting was headed by two workers, late Ernest Nelson being one. Instead of the workers encouraging us to ask them questions, they immediately went into a tirade criticizing us for being involved in too many worldly activities, robbing us of valuable time studying the scriptures. They were critical of recreational sports, such as skiing, skating, playing soccer, etc. I apparently stood to my feet expounding the virtues of such activities. The workers gave me no answers but stared me down into my seat. This was the last time I ever participated in a meeting.*[201]

---

[200]   Chapman, *Reflections*, 194.
[201]   Email 17th February 2012.

One young man who has left and worships in a Baptist church in the US writes, 'extra biblical traditions that must not be broken. These include engagement rings, long hair, strictly home-based churches, no consumption of alcohol (although addictions to sugar, coffee, work, hobbies was ok).'[202] The members live under a cloud of fear that they are failing to reach the standards set for them by the workers. 'Unworthy' in 2x2 terminology means failure to live up to what is expected from them as members of the movement. Fortt elucidates this when he writes:

> *The idea is probably best expressed by the fact that everyone knows full well that being a member of "The Truth" holds much suffering in store, yet every member sees it as "God's wonderful Way," where there is 'great joy' in perpetual misery. Members and workers talk of love, yet judge each other severely; they talk of freedom while in bondage to the "unwritten law".*[203]

The prayers and testimonies at conventions are evidence of the fear and bondage that seem to grip these people. It is difficult to equate this with the joy that accompanies salvation. Parker captures this when he writes, 'the concept that assurance of salvation is dependent upon personal merit causes much strain and may be linked to the emotion that has been observed in members' prayers at conventions and house sect meetings for strength "to keep faithful to the way."'[204] Examples of these are, 'our Father I thank thee that we have the privilege to be here, to be thy Children, to hear thy voice and know that thou hast softened our hearts and drawn each one of us close to thee and to this Jesus again we ask and help us just to follow in Jesus name. Amen.'[205] Another testified, 'so much made me think that I am here because others have prayed for me and because God hasn't let me go easily. And He hasn't let me leave without a struggle and without a fight and you know without that I'd be quite far from here today.'[206]

Members are very fearful that they may upset a worker even

---

[202] Email 9th February 2012.
[203] Fortt, *Search for "the Truth"*, 186.
[204] Parker, *Secret Sect*, 101.
[205] Cork Convention, Saturday morning, June 2010.
[206] Fermanagh convention, Sunday morning, June 2010.

inadvertently. During this research, I have had a number of anonymous calls from those who wanted to express their views but were afraid to do it openly. Many who emailed had the same fear and requested anonymity. To express a view openly which is even mildly in disagreement would transgress the rules and lead to excommunication.

Workers

'Worker' is the term given to their ministers and for those who pride themselves on always using biblical terminology this is certainly one that would be difficult to sustain. A former university lecturer who was born into a 2x2 family comments, 'if ever there was a misnomer it is the term worker because work is not something any of them do.'[207] When asked to expand on this she said:

> *My father and mother were devout 2x2s and my uncle was an overseer. Consequently, I was able to observe the movement and their workers at close quarters. As a child, my brother and I were forced to give up our beds so that workers could stay in our house for months at a time. They were supposed to spend time reading their Bibles and praying but I saw little of that and they never offered to help in the house but expected their meals on time. I was always puzzled by their relaxed lifestyle and that they were waited on at every turn.[208]*

Workers generally come from families who have a long history within the movement and many of the younger workers, those under forty years, are third or fourth generation. Many go into the work at around twenty years old but some begin later than this. Females usually enter the work later than males. Some of these have third level education and will have trained as teachers or nurses but none will have any training or educational background of a theological nature. There is always a note of disdain in the voice of a worker when they refer to theological training. This attitude is traceable to the early days of the movement. Of the early workers Parker comments, 'many were poorly educated

---

[207] Discussion in Manchester, 12th October 2011.
[208] Discussion in Manchester, 12th October 2011.

but they were assured that anyone could become a preacher. Prejudice against education formed part of the antipathy to the clergy and to the privileged rich, and convention goers were told that learning could be a hindrance to the truth.'[209] There is a distinct aversion to change as noted from the sermon by a Fermanagh convention speaker, David Delaney, who when talking on the book of Nehemiah referred to the Old Gate and said:

> There is one it mentions the Old Gate and I like this and it was briefly mentioned in Monaghan but it appealed to me again about the old gate. It talks about not to put away the ancient landmarks and in Jeremiah it talks about where is the old way and let us walk therein and this way of God [the 2x2 movement] is not in a position to be modernised. It isn't in a position to have new thinking. It doesn't need learned, educated men to prove that things are different now because we are talking about an old established word of God. As we heard in Monaghan it is forever set in the way. It is the old way. The old gate, the ancient landmark, the things that are forever settled in heaven…In spite of the modernisations, in spite of everything that this ministry works. We have proved it, we have proved that the simple homeless ministry having left everything and interestingly just talking to someone recently he made the comment, 'I never realised that workers don't have bank accounts.'[210]

It is difficult to understand this rather novel application of this text that the speaker uses to resist change in the movement, reject education and extoll the 2x2 form of ministry. From a sociological viewpoint, it seems odd to make a virtue out of the fact that 'workers don't have bank accounts'. Given that most of these workers travel to other parts of the world, sometimes as a longer-term mission and at other times to speak at conventions, the lack of a bank account would be a serious imposition. We know that most if not all airlines require a credit or a bank debit card to book flights but that is not an insurmountable

[209] Parker, *Secret Sect*, 17.
[210] Fermanagh Convention. June 2011. Saturday morning, David Delaney. In a discussion with an ex-worker who left the work in 2010, he told me that he and most other workers he knew had bank accounts and credit cards.

problem since some airlines will permit others to book flights on behalf of the traveller. What happens with the airlines who insist that the traveller uses their own card and uses the card as a means of validating their identity at the airport? Speaking at the Fermanagh convention, one worker, Herbie Eaton, related his experience of staying in a hotel in West Africa and watching the events of the aircraft hitting the twin towers unfolding in New York. He justifies the workers staying in the hotel because there were no friends [their members] in the area to provide accommodation. This raises two issues, the first is that staying in hotels usually requires credit cards as a guarantee for any extras and since there were no 'friends' in the area to settle the bill, they must have had some means to do this and this hardly points to the penniless worker. The second issue being that 2x2s strongly oppose either owning or viewing television so how does he justify watching the unfolding of these events?[211]

An important ethical issue emerges from the idea that 'workers don't have bank accounts'. Workers pay no taxes on the gifts they receive from members to provide for daily provisions. It is of course much more difficult to track down the amount of gift income a worker receives when gifts are in cash and there is no bank account to provide an audit trail. Since the law in most countries requires everyone to pay taxes on income over a certain level can we believe that these workers are operating with transparency when it comes to their income? They are not following the injunction of Scripture, 'Render therefore unto Caesar the things which be Caesar's, and unto God the things which be God's' (Luke 20:25). One former member wrote the following:

> *The system encourages and practices a degree of lawlessness, in its concealment of its operations and financial dealings and its arrangement for its clergy members not to pay taxes and some of the laity to collude with the clergy [workers] to make this possible, and its games concerning the uses and ownership of convention grounds, again evading numerous laws that apply to the rest of society and which they have no honest reason to evade. Meanwhile, workers, who do not contribute to funding social programs, do use those programs, for*

> *health care and housing, and are supported by government programs*
> *such as HUD [Housing and Urban Development] and waivered*
> *care and visiting nurses and food stamps and energy assistance and*
> *cash assistance. Everyone who is involved in such connivance is part*
> *of an elaborate system that uses mind control and social pressure to*
> *enforce collaboration and secrecy.[212]*

This statement is a serious indictment of friends and workers who apparently collude in wholesale corruption and hardly befits those who claim to follow the example of Jesus. These homeless workers live on gifts provided by the members and are always assured of comfortable lodgings. These are prepared well in advance in the homes of the faithful. In a discussion with an elderly 'professing' woman she commented, naming the worker, 'he is coming to stay with us all of next week.'[213] In a meeting with two Irish workers, one of them commented regarding their staying in members' homes, 'we have more homes than we can reach on'. I asked, 'surely the 'more homes than you can reach on' negates the faith principle in going out not knowing whither you are going? I used the example of the twelve apostles in Matthew 10 in that when they were going out they certainly could not say where they were staying weeks ahead.

The senior worker felt my question on faith was irrelevant and he used the example of him arriving in County Armagh where he had never worked before and receiving invitations from folk he had never met before. He thinks that it is by faith when you go to a new area these things happen. He is of the opinion that it is what we read of in the New Testament. It would be difficult to construe the certainty of food and accommodation well into the future as demonstrating a life lived by faith that God alone will provide.

One could quite easily pass male workers off as executives in their well-cut suits, shirts and ties, sometimes with designer labels. Workers see themselves as making a big sacrifice and that being homeless somehow gives them special status but there is nothing in their appearance that

---

[212] Email 19th November 2011.
[213] Personal discussion Friday 7th October 2011.

suggests that they do not enjoy a comfortable lifestyle. An interesting observation over the three days spent at the Swedish convention was that workers, male and female, had several changes of clothing and that hardly meets with the Matthew 10 model of ministry. Most workers have mobile phones and a large number, especially the younger ones, have laptops and certainly show no appearance of being financially disadvantaged. They all have use of cars provided by members.

From time to time during sermons, a worker will refer to the struggle when deciding whether or not to go into the work. There seems little evidence from these comments that there is an assurance that they are responding to the call of God but more of responding to what may be expected from their peers. An experienced worker, Herbie Jennings[214] related his battle before submitting as a worker:

> *I remember this platform, it was a different one I'm sure, I remember that door. . . I asked God to convict, I asked that. . . I didn't want to go do the work, I didn't want to do this preaching of the gospel, it didn't suit me, it didn't suit my nature, but I was afflicted to do it for years. And it was getting to the stage now I was going to lose my peace so I had do something. I prayed earnestly that I would come here that the workers, visiting workers, would give their testimony, about the work. And it happened in the first meeting and happened in the second and happened in the third meeting, you know this is no coincidence, God does hear prayer, God will answer prayer it's God's doings. . . But I didn't realize I still remember I was sitting in here, down there in the next meeting and uncle Irvine [Pearson] stood up here to speak, I didn't know he was speaking and he said I'm going to say something, he said I've been trying to get away from it, but he I've nothing else to tell you. And he gave his own experience about going to work. . . It was very easy, it wasn't easy for him to speak and it wasn't easy for some of us to listen either. But it was just a real experience, I'm only mentioning this because you know, this work is of God, this thing is of God.[215]*

---

[214] Full transcript of Jennings' decision to go into the work in appendix 4, page 168.
[215] Cork Convention, Saturday morning June 2010.

This is only the story of one worker and other workers have related similar struggles in reaching a decision to go into the work.[216] Although they talk a lot about God's will there is rarely any Scripture used to support the idea of a call. These struggles and subsequent delays in going into the work stand in sharp contrast to Jesus' calling of the apostles whom they claim to emulate. Jesus called Peter and Andrew 'and they straightway left their nets, and followed him' (Matthew 5:20). He then called James and John 'and immediately left the ship and their father, and followed him' (Matthew 5:22).

The life of a worker is one where they are highly esteemed by the laity. They lead lives that are distant and removed from the day-to-day problems of real life. Stone summarises this succinctly, saying that, 'the workers live in even more of a bubble than the friends do. They are not required to interact with the world at all and can't (sic) relate to real life in any sort of a practical way. The workers actually live a monastic sort of life even though they are surrounded by others who must participate in the activities of life.'[217] Conventions illustrate the gap between workers and members, when workers eat together, sleep in separate quarters and during meetings sit in comfortable seats especially reserved. Jennings spoke of his first convention as a worker:

The first time I ever slept in the workers hall, where the workers were gathered. I went to Downpatrick convention, I got a phone call to say I was going to be on the list[218], didn't (sic) know where I was going to be. So I went off to Downpatrick convention and met Willie Wilken in the yard and I was going off with my sleeping stuff and Willie says where are going? I said I'm going such and such a place to sleep. Oh no you're not he said, you're going down to the brothers [workers] hall where the other workers are sleeping. I'd never been down there before. I couldn't, I couldn't, it was a bad start to say to uncle Willie I can't go, I'm not going. So I went down there and I walked in through that door and there was seven or eight brother workers there.[219]

<hr>

[216] Discussion accompanied by my son David with two workers, 20th January 2012.
[217] Stone, *Church Without A Name*, 63.
[218] The list is the names of workers in a region and is decided by the head worker who will inform one who has indicated that they are called to the work when they are selected.
[219] Herbie Jennings, Cork Convention, June 2010.

Observing the interaction between workers and laity one can detect subservience on the part of the laity that gives the impression that workers are on a pedestal. The hierarchy is evident from the top down with laity and junior workers referring to the older workers as uncle and auntie. When one becomes a worker, they commit themselves to submitting to the authority of the overseer of the area where they work. Overseers will not tolerate any worker stepping out of line and in an organisation where there is no written statement of beliefs or policies, this must be difficult. Workers are dismissed or excommunicated and very often without any satisfactory explanation to fellow workers or members. I attended the Fermanagh convention in June 2010 and one worker whom I have known since childhood was on the convention speakers' rota but a few weeks later his name was not on the workers list. This worker aged in his mid-sixties had spent his life in the work. He was born into a 2x2 family where his father was a worker at one time. In the area of Fermanagh and Tyrone rumours abound as to why he is no longer a worker and even senior members with whom I have spoken are unsure as to the circumstances.

One senior member confided that there are rumblings of discontent over the matter and that overseers often act in an autocratic way instead of applying the New Testament methods of church discipline. There is a litany of stories from ex-workers who have left the work or been excommunicated. One such account comes from a Washington, US resident, Dennis Jacobsen, a sixty-eight year old whose profile appears on the 'truth message boards' (TMB).[220] His account is published in detail in *Reflections*[221] Jacobsen was raised in devout believer lifestyle having professed at age eleven years and baptised at fifteen years old. He writes:

> *Once I was, perhaps like you are yet, a fully dedicated and fully persuaded believer of a fellowship group which I knew only as "the Truth" from birth. As such, I thought the system, method, fellowship was of Divine, rather than human origins, and therefore "perfect". You have the testimonies of many claiming it is and works "perfect;"*

---

[220] Jacobsen's profile on TMB. He has sent me a private message permitting me to use his postings in this research. 21st December 2011.

[221] Chapman, *Reflections*, 266-276.

none dare say it is not your right to know how, when and where others believe it has failed completely. In this collection of compositions you will read of a number of such times and occurrences. Like others, my account is true and factual.[222]

He entered the work in 1966 and served in the United States and Sweden before leaving in 1986. This is a précis of Jacobsen's account:

In 1986 as a young worker he became aware of happenings with which he disagreed. These included a power hungry overseer who grabbed power and was not appointed; a semi overseer who was having sexual relations with six female workers and a homosexual worker seeking to remain in the work. Soon he was falsely accused, excommunicated, lied about, libelled and slandered worldwide by the three men who put him out of the work to cover their wickedness.

He has never had an apology, never a sign of remorse, never an offer of restoration or reconciliation despite initial years attempting such. He knows what goes on in that group and how they defend the indefensible. Current exposures have been only a tip of an iceberg existing through the years. He is thankful for what he had to go through to discover what was really true about "the truth" and many of its workers. Those defending them, now as then, merely reveal how little they really know themselves. It has been over 25 years and it has not changed one iota. On the other hand, the false accusations against him have changed so many times.[223]

Many stories with a similar tenor abound and show the hierarchy, fellow workers and members as ruthless and insensitive. Another example of this is the excommunication of ex-worker, Edgar Massey and his family in 2001, after he raised concerns following a number of incidents that undermined his trust in the movement. Massey from Saskatchewan, Canada writes, 'I was in the work 8 years before coming here to Sweden where I was in the work 8 more years.'[224] Massey has written his story in detail and it is published in full on the web. He explains:

[222] Chapman, *Reflections*, 266.
[223] http://professing.proboards.com/index.cgi?action=display&board=general&thread=1852 0&page=1. Accessed 3rd February 2012.
[224] Facebook message, 18th June 2011.

My credentials in 2x2ism were likely as impeccable as exist in the 2x2 measurement system. I was born and raised under the full influence of the system . . . in 1981 I fell in love with a girl that came to our meetings, and decided to leave the work and get married. This caused a bit of a fuss in the group at the time – but the fuss subsided fairly quickly as we established an 'open home' (which are very very scarce in Sweden). . . The miracle of the Red sea has been a tremendous comfort to me.. First, the door of escape for us was presented by the workers themselves. I am doubtful if I could have found my way out of the 2x2 culture on my own – but the door of banishment gave us a passage out that only gave us the 'one option'. Looking back on it, we are convinced it was arranged by God himself.

Then equally marvellous was the closing of the sea behind us – There was an enormous campaign by the workers to discredit us, slander us, and to 'wipe us off the map' – but shortly after our rejection we experienced the wonderful beauty of the complete 'sealing off' of this disconcerting influence of the cult from our lives. Once the initial 'bubbles in the pot' had subsided, we haven't had a visit from a single worker in our home – five years have gone by now. Very, very few of our former 2x2 friends have even answered our phone calls – Our exit through the sea seems to have consumed them all!! .. from our perspective at least. A few 'borderline' friends have dared to call on us – In the 5 years, we have been to 3 or 4 funerals where workers are involved – but that is it![225]

Particularly in the United States of America the 2x2s have suffered from adverse publicity because of some workers who committed sexual offences against children. The headline in the Huron Daily Tribune, Michigan on 9th February read, 'Briggs sentenced to jail time for CSC' and the report revealed:

A 36-year-old New York man on Monday was sentenced to 180 days in jail for a fourth-degree criminal sexual conduct charge stemming from an incident that occurred in November 2006 with a then-11-year-old boy living in the Bingham Township home where

---

[225] An excerpt from Edgar Massey's account published on http://www.anotherstep.net/ourstory/.

the man had been staying through a non-denominational Christian organization [2x2]. . . During Monday's sentencing, a charge against Darren Jay Briggs, 36, of Syracuse, N.Y.[226]

One Irish worker in the eighties abused several young boys in Northern Ireland and when this was reported to the overseer and workers he was quietly moved to work in the Republic of Ireland where he was out of reach of the (then) Royal Ulster Constabulary, should it become a police matter. Noel Tanner who was from Cork subsequently left the work in 1983 and his future activities brought two convictions in the Republic of Ireland for sexual offences. Reports of these offences appeared in the press.[227] The full story relating to Tanner's offences against the boys in Northern Ireland was written by one of the victims[228] and appears on a website.[229]

Allocation of workers to various fields within a territory is, I am informed, done arbitrarily by the head worker for the territory at the end of the convention in the region. For example, the Stockholm convention in July 2011 was the last in the Scandinavian territory. The postings were announced showing where each of the workers would serve from August to December 2011. There are eleven workers in Sweden of which three are from the United States, one from Canada and one from Ireland. There are eight workers in Finland of which four are from the United States. There are thirteen workers in Norway of which two are from Canada, one from Russia and one from the United States. Denmark has seven workers, all nationals. The list shows the workers' names, contact addresses and telephone numbers, all of which points to a behind the scenes organisation.

---

[226] http://www.michigansthumb.com/articles/2010/02/09/news/police_-_courts/doc4b715c17bc564579368752.txt. Accessed 3rd February 2012.

[227] http://www.wingsfortruth.info/noeltanner.pdf. Transcript of the report from *Cork Examiner*, January 1991.

[228] I met this victim on two occasions – last time on 15th February 2012 and he gave permission to use this posting.

[229] http://www.wingsfortruth.info/robertkee.pdf. I have met and spoken with the victim.

In the past workers were ordained[230] a 'Minister of the Gospel' at conventions. The print below confirms this and they were using the name of 'The United Christian Conventions of Australasia and New Zealand'. We could not ascertain if this practice still operates when it is judged 'expedient' but this evidence certainly undermines the idea of 'a church without a name'.

Workers who give the impression of being subservient are generally very demanding and are always determined that their word is law. It is difficult to envisage any other scenario where a person without any training, theological or pastoral, is given such blind allegiance as is evident in the worker/friend relationship.

....

230   Reference and certification that Ron Campbell was an Ordained Minister with this fellowship, dated April 20, 1928. Signed by William John Hughes, Overseer. http://www.tellingthetruth.info/plogger/?level=picture&id=293. Accessed 10th April 2012.

Sociological Critique

When one observes how seamlessly all of the activities fall into place on a worldwide scale then the idea that it is without organisation fades away. Conventions lists published for every location and the logistics of organising the workers who will speak at each convention and their travel plans defy the notion that this is all without a secret headquarters. For example, the 2008 list[231] shows 452 conventions held in a range of countries, Europe, Asia, South America, USA, Canada, Australia and New Zealand.

There may not be a single presidential style figure in control but it is naïve to think that there is no one in control to ensure that events run smoothly. An example of such control is found in the Acts of the Apostles where there was a council in Jerusalem to whom the apostles reported and who decided on matters of doctrine and controversy. Why then can they not acknowledge that such a hierarchy has a precedent in Scripture?

The lack of a hierarchy leads to lack of accountability by members, workers and overseers with everyone doing what is right in his own eyes. Overseers are often autocratic and unapproachable and make decisions that are quite often against the will of the majority. One elderly member confirmed this in a telephone discussion.[232] This is particularly evident in the mishandling of child sex abuse and a current case going through the courts in the US shows the lengths to which overseers are prepared to go, to abdicate responsibility. The overseer was charged for not reporting the case to the authorities and as a defence states that he is not an ordained minister.[233]

This organization is self-centred with concern only for the well-being of its workers and members and without regard for the problems of the outside world. The most glaring example of this was at the Stockholm convention held 21st to 24th July 2011. A terrible massacre happened

---

[231] http://www.votisalive.com/content/worldwide-convention-list-2008-here-accurate-count-2x2-conventions. Accessed 29th February 2012.

[232] Telephone discussion 28th February 2012.

[233] http://www.2x2ministry.org/Jerome_Frandle/jerome_frandle_criminal_pretrial.php.

in Norway on Friday 22ⁿᵈ July when more than eighty, mainly young people lost their lives. The morning 2x2 convention commenced on Saturday 24ᵗʰ July without a prayer or a word of concern for those who had lost loved ones in the tragedy. The silence on that terrible event was palpable and particularly relevant given that there were a number of Norwegians at the convention.

They are oblivious to those who are underprivileged and stigmatized by society. They have no concept of how Jesus defines a 'neighbour'. When he was asked 'who is my neighbour?' (Luke 10:29) Jesus responded by telling the parable of the Good Samaritan (Luke 10: 30-37). Unlike the 2x2s who will only provide help and assistance to those with whom they are in fellowship Jesus is pointing out that 'neighbour' crosses all social and racial barriers. One former worker commented, 'the workers do not do any significant charitable work in the communities as they have a doctrine of not wanting "rice Christians". They use the verse "The poor you have always with you" to justify not giving to the poor.'[234]

Dysfunctional is a word that springs to mind when analysing the sociological aspects of the movement. There is a lack of coherence and rational thought from the top down albeit that they deny the existence of a hierarchy. An example of this is the handling of issues such as divorce and remarriage and the differing opinions of overseers and workers. Their unwritten rules serve to create an unhealthy atmosphere of fear and bondage with members always hoping that they are doing right.

One former member writes, 'salvation [is] based on church attendance. If you did not go to meeting without valid reasons, you were seen as struggling.[235] From an evangelical perspective a 2x2 member never has any assurance of their salvation and one former member writes, 'ask a 2x2 if they are saved they will say, "I hope so", or "I'm trying to be". Works are everything.'[236] This mentality perpetuates fear and insecurity. Reading the personal accounts in *Reflections* and *Reflected Truth* of those who left the movement or were excommunicated and the harsh and

[234] http://professing.proboards.com/index.cgi?board=general&action=display&thread=1871 8&page=2. Accessed 22ⁿᵈ February 2012.
[235] Email 9ᵗʰ February 2012.
[236] Email 21ˢᵗ March 2012.

insensitive treatment from those at all levels in the movement including those who hitherto were close friends and family is frightening. In addition, in the course of this research a large number came forward with emails of the most harrowing stories of abuses of the most vile kind that were ignored when reported to workers or overseers and in some cases parents. Workers condemn as apostates those who write their accounts. This is a major misuse of the word apostate.

Those who are born into a 2x2 family are ill-equipped to face the outside world in that they have been brainwashed[237] into believing that the movement is the only custodian of gospel truth. As one forty year old women writes, 'after I quit meetings, one thing that kept me from going back is realizing how sheltered and unprepared I'd been for the "real world" growing up in Truth.'[238] This is a typical reaction of those born into a 2x2 family and eventually leave following negative experiences.

One former member who left thirty years ago writes, 'I believe that it is a cult because of the "mind control" that is attempted. There are not supposed to be any questions, obedience and following the utterances of the "men of god" is utmost. Social contact with outsiders is discouraged.'[239] This is only one of many similar comments I have received during this research and from a sociological perspective, it raises legitimate concerns at the damage done by this group largely because of the claims of exclusivity and the arbitrary decisions that are not open to question. The lack of accountability and transparency leads to confusion at all levels and especially amongst the members.

---

[237] Meeting with a former member in Manchester, 22nd March 2012, she claims there is a strong element of mind control.
[238] Email 16th November 2011.
[239] Email 23rd November 2011.

The Theology Of The 2x2 Movement

Trying to construct a detailed theology of the 2x2s is exceedingly difficult for two reasons. The first is the absence of a written record stating what they believe. The second is that when pressed as to their beliefs they sidestep the issue. 'They claim to have no doctrine and refuse to formally publish any other than to state that they believe and follow the teachings of the New Testament.'[240] For example, one can examine the theology of Presbyterianism from a study of the Westminster Confession of Faith; the Anglican Church from a study of the Thirty-Nine Articles of Faith or a local Baptist Church will have a statement of beliefs and doctrines. The absence of any such statement of beliefs and doctrines by the 2x2 movement creates a vacuum that gives overseers and workers *carte blanche* and ends up with *ad hoc* rules, beliefs and ethics.

An important starting point to begin the study of the 2x2 theology are the views of the early leaders and an extract from Long's diary from March 1898 helpfully summarises William Irvine's view:

> *Concerning the principles of the Doctrine of Christ, he was sound. He believed in the fall of man, in the Atonement, in the Trinity, in the Divinity of our Lord, in the immortality of the soul, in the resurrection of the body, the inspiration of the Bible, in Heaven for the saved, and in Hell for the lost. He believed in a personal Devil, the enemy of God and man. He believed and taught Repentance and that every person can be saved and know it, and that the conditions of Salvation were "If thou shalt confess with thy mouth the Lord Jesus, and shalt believe in thine heart that God hath raised Him from the dead, thou shalt be saved." Romans 10:9. He taught that every saved soul is indwelt by the Spirit of Christ; and that the life of Jesus, is the pattern for everyone to imitate and follow; and that the life of forsaking all for Christ's sake was the best to live. The fruits of that teaching resulted in farmers, shop keepers, domestic servants, school teachers, police, soldiers, and persons of every occupation forsaking all that they had to follow Jesus; and to preach the Gospel of the Kingdom of God.*[241]

....
[240]   Daniel, *Reinventing The Truth*, 18.
[241]   John Long's diary.

Based on that short assessment one could certainly deduce that at least Irvine subscribed to the basics of the traditional Christian faith. On reading Long's statement, it clearly incorporates the four characteristics of evangelicalism – the Bible, the cross, conversion and activism. If this was an accurate reflection of what Irvine believed and was the starting point for the movement there is evidence that this quickly changed. This is no longer the basis for their *modus operandi* some one hundred years later. Long's statement lists three important doctrines that undergird the characteristics of evangelicalism – the deity of Christ, the Trinity and the atonement. The doctrine of Christ surely includes the 'Divinity of our Lord', the atonement and the Trinity are all important pillars of the Christian faith but aspects of these are denied or at best trivialised by the 2x2 movement.

On the importance of the deity of Christ and the atonement, McGrath writes, 'for evangelicalism, Jesus Christ is of central importance. He is the focal point of Scripture. He alone possessed the unique distinction of being at one and the same time "true God and true man." Through his atoning death alone we have access to God.'[242] On the significance of the Trinity Stott writes, 'it is God himself, the Holy Trinity, who causes conversion, promotes evangelism and creates fellowship.'[243]

This section will examine these doctrines and other 2x2 beliefs and finally reach conclusions based on the findings. Parker's view does not concur with Long's assessment. Parker writes, 'Irvine had no time for those who preached trust in Christ as redeemer of men, "the Calvary ranters", as he called them.'[244]

Parker points out, 'the doctrinal position of the sect has not been found to be consistent with what it has been represented to be, and, as in the matter of doctrine, the sect has not provided factual statements of its history and beliefs, the facts having been disguised through the medium of preacher control.'[245]

....

[242]   McGrath, *Evangelicalism*, 61
[243]   Stott, *Evangelical Truth*, 28.
[244]   Parker, *Secret Sect*, 19.
[245]   Parker, *Secret Sect*, 105.

Use Of New Testament

Many of the 2x2s, especially those outside Ireland and the United Kingdom, believe that they have an unbroken line of succession from the New Testament Church on the shores of Galilee. They continue to follow the model of ministry found in Matthew 10 and advocated by Irvine and Cooney and all of those workers of the early twentieth century. To help understand the movement and to put it in context it is important to consider it within the framework of the New Testament and early church. We have access to both internal evidence in the Scriptures and external evidence from the early church fathers and secular history. Describing the early church Caird posits:

> *The first Christians were men with a story to tell, which was so important that they were ready to risk persecution and death in the telling of it. It was the story of Jesus, a man whom many of them had known intimately during the last tumultuous years that led up to his death, a man who after his death had appeared alive to many witnesses. But as they told the story, it was above all a story about God. . . This story was called the Gospel (evangelion).*[246]

In 2x2 preaching there is constant reference to the gospel but there is never an explanation as to what the gospel is. From their preaching, it would be difficult to infer that the story they tell is that of the Christian gospel. There is nothing in 2x2 preaching that matches Caird's description of the first Christians. Because the 2x2s hold that their form of church and ministry emanated from the New Testament Church, it is important that we consider the early church and its mission during the formative days. Commenting on the Church following Pentecost in Acts 2:42-47 Stott outlines some of their important features:

1. It was a learning church - *they devoted themselves to the apostles' teaching.*

2. It was a loving church - *they devoted themselves to the fellowship (koinõnia).* Koinõnia (from koinos, (common) bears witness to the

---

[246]   Caird, G. B, *The Apostolic Age*, (London: Duckworth, 1955), 36.

common life of the church in two senses.[247]

3. It was a worshipping church – *they devoted themselves . . . to the breaking of bread and prayer.* That is, their fellowship was expressed not only in caring for each other, but in corporate worship too.

4. It was an evangelistic church – *and the Lord added to their number daily those who were being saved.*[248]

Against the criteria of the early church, it would be difficult for any church to claim that their church mirrors the New Testament church. Nevertheless, the 2x2s are adamant that they and they alone have what they call 'the Truth' and that their model of church is the only one that is correct. One can only come to faith in Christ through the preaching of one of their workers.

Tidball makes a valid point when he writes,

> *The early church was an imperfect church. It faced all the challenges of an emerging church without any experience or precedence to fall back on. It is evident that they did not always get things right, at least initially. . . So in terms of leadership there is wisdom from which we can benefit, even if it does not present a blueprint we should automatically adopt.*[249]

The New Testament canon provides us with sufficient evidence to help us build an accurate picture of the early church but we must be aware of other religious and secular writings from this period that help complete the picture. There are the four Gospels and one subject – the Lord Jesus Christ. Of course the ministry of Jesus as presented in the Gospels and of the apostles and Paul in the Book of Acts is of vital importance. The epistles of Paul and others in the New Testament give an insight into the situation in the various New Testament churches

---

[247] On the two senses, Stott writes, first, it expresses what we share together. That is God himself, for 'our fellowship is with the Father and his Son, Jesus Christ', and then there is 'the fellowship of the Holy Spirit. Thus, *koinōnia* is a Trinitarian experience; it is our common share in God, Father, Son and Holy Spirit. Secondly, *koinōnia* also expresses what we share out together, what we give as well as what we receive. Stott, John, *The Message of Acts*, (Leicester: IVP, 1990), 82-83.

[248] Stott, *Acts*, 82-83.

[249] Tidball, *Ministry by the Book*, 87.

and give clear guidance as to the practices and teachings of the church. Most scholars agree that the writings of the New Testament were complete before the end of the first century. However, scholars agree that the final canon of Scripture as we know it today was much later than this. According to one source, 'in one sense the canon was closed around 95 when the book of Revelation was written as the last book to be included in the canon of NT . . . individual NT books were settled through a process of deliberation until one finds a virtual consensus regarding the contents of the canon of the NT in the fourth century.'[250] The first fully extant listing we have is in Athanasius's *Festal Letter* of 367.

It is important to recognise that the formulation of the New Testament was not an arbitrary action on the part of the church and Bray points out:

> *The apostles evidently were conscious of possessing a teaching authority in the church, which was given to them by Jesus himself (Eph. 2:20; Gal 1:8-9; 2 Cor. 11-12). Later generations accepted this to the extent of restricting entry into the canon to those books that could be shown to have been received in the church as authentically apostolic, either because they had been written by an apostle or because they had been composed under the direction of one.*[251]

The Christians for the first few centuries did not have the benefits of immediate access to the New Testament Scriptures as we do today. Therefore, it would have been difficult for the 2x2s to claim or garner evidence that Matthew 10, Mark 6 or Luke 9 and 10 were the only model for ministry or that the church in the home was the only place to worship. In Scripture we do not find a command from Jesus in support for the church in the home. The 2x2s will point to the accounts of the institution of the Lord's Supper in Matthew 26:17-19; Mark 14:12-16 and Luke 22:7-13 as support that Jesus ordained the church in the home but even a cursory reading of these passages would suggest that such an interpretation is tenuous at best.

....

[250] Köstenberger, Andreas, Kellum, L Scott. and Quarles, Charles L, *The Cradle, The Cross and The Crown,* (Nashville: B&H Publishing, 2009), 30.

[251] Bray, Gerald, *Biblical Interpretation,* (Downers Grove: IVP, 1996), 30.

The Old Testament was the only Scripture available to the emerging first-century church. We have confirmation of this in Paul's letter to Timothy: 'And that from a child thou hast known the holy scriptures, which are able to make thee wise unto salvation through faith which is Christ Jesus' (2 Timothy 3:15). Paul can only be referring to the Old Testament scriptures. From the beginning there was no doubt that the Old Testament had to be preserved. The Old Testament was not only the Holy Scripture of Jesus and the apostles, but the source cited by Paul several times throughout his writings. Aland writes, 'quite simply, the Old Testament was the holy document of the time. Even until the third generation, whenever Christians were asked for written documents of their faith, without exception they unambiguously pointed first to the Old Testament.'[252]

It is important to distinguish between what is descriptive and what is prescriptive in Scripture. For example, there are some who think that the Great Commission (Matthew 28:18-20; Mark 16:15; Luke 24:46-49; Acts 1:7-8) is descriptive but it would be difficult to support that viewpoint since this was meant to apply to followers of Christ in all ages and not only those who heard it directly from the Lord himself. Stott comments, 'in seeking to live for Christ we are concerned to do His will and keep his commandments, all of them. We are not at liberty to pick and choose. Nor do we wish to. So we must not overlook his last commandment, to 'go . . . and make disciples.''[253] In contrast to this the sending of the twelve in Matthew 10 to the house of Israel should be viewed as descriptive simply because there is no way that this can be repeated. Nevertheless, it is this passage of Scripture that Irvine and Cooney and today's 2x2s use to support their model of ministry. Wilson comments:

> *Obviously the injunctions of Matthew 10 are not the entire substance of the Cooneyite teaching, but they provide the raison d'être for Go-preachers, and thus justify others in receiving them and supporting them. The role of this preaching class, and its relation to the Cooneyite following is, of course, one of the distinctive features of the movement.*[254]

---

[252] Kurt Aland, *A History of Christianity*, (Philadelphia, Fortress Press, English Translation, 1985), 76.
[253] Stott, John, *Our Guilty Silence*, (Leicester: IVP, 1997), 18.
[254] Parker, *Secret Sect*, xi.

From a theological viewpoint, Hammond writes:

> *The advocates of this body contend that the injunctions in Matthew 10 are directed for (sic) the whole of Christ's followers and for all time. They ignore the command, 'Go not into the way of the Gentiles, and into any of the city of the Samaritans enter ye not, which plainly indicates the temporary nature of this particular commission to the twelve.*[255]

Model Of Matthew 10:5-15

From the earliest accounts, we find that Matthew chapter 10 played a major role in the establishment of the movement's practices and beliefs. There is little doubt that the distinctives of the movement are the homeless, unsalaried workers (preachers) and the church that meets in the home. As a basis for their homeless, unsalaried worker they point to Matthew 10:5-15:

"5 These twelve Jesus sent forth, and commanded them, saying, Go not into the way of the Gentiles, and any city of the Samaritans enter ye not. 6 But go rather to the lost sheep of the house of Israel. 7 And as you go, preach, saying, the kingdom of heaven is at hand. 8 Heal the sick, cleanse the lepers, raise the dead, cast out devils: freely ye have received, freely give. 9 Provide neither Gold, nor silver, nor brass in your purses, 10 Nor Scrip for your journey, neither two coats, neither shoes, nor yet staves; for the workman is worthy of his meat. 11 And into whatsoever city or town ye shall enter, enquire who in it is worthy; and there abide till ye go thence. 12 And when ye come into a house, salute it. 13 And if the house be worthy, let your peace come upon it: but if it be not worthy, let your peace return to you. 14 And whosoever shall not receive you, nor hear your words, when ye depart out of that house or city, shake off the dust off your feet. 15 Verily I say unto you, it shall be tolerable for the land of Sodom and Gomorrha[256] in the day of judgement, than for that city."

---

[255] Hammond Statement.
[256] This spelling is peculiar to some editions of the KJV. Spelt Gomorrah in NIV, ESV and RSV.

One of the movement's first workers was Irvine Weir who wrote:

> *William Irvine's ideas of preaching and tramp preaching were founded entirely on his idea of the tenth Matthew (sic) where Jesus told them to go, providing themselves neither gold nor silver nor script or staff for their journey, neither two coats, neither shoes nor staves for the workman is worthy of his hire. William believed that what was good for the apostles was also good for the preachers of that day. He forgot that this message was given to the apostles to give to the Jewish nation only.*[257]

Cooney too believed that the commission given to the twelve apostles in Matthew 10 was a permanent one for his sent ones for all ages. Roberts writes, 'Edward Cooney believed that there was only one way for the apostles or sent ones to go to preach; that was the way Jesus went and the way he sent the 12 and the 70, with no provision except from God.'[258] Roberts acknowledges the argument that Matthew 10 was a mission only to the house of Israel and that this was only a temporary commission and subsequently different instructions were given in Luke 22: 35-36. Roberts writes, 'This argument was constantly being brought up against Edward and his fellow preachers; but they were able to refute it from Scripture.'[259] There is no evidence of his rebuttal.

When we examine the preaching of Irvine and Cooney we find they used Matthew 10 as the basis for the new movement and even in the twenty-first century preachers still refer to the significance of this passage to support their idea of the workers being homeless and without any source of income apart from gifts provided by their adherents. It is therefore important in the context of Scripture to examine Matthew 10 on three counts:

1. The nature of the mission

2. The basis for idea of the homeless, unsalaried worker

3. The 2x2s' selective fulfilment of Matthew 10

[257] Parker Doug and Helen, *Secret Sect*, 9. A personal letter to Doug Parker from Irvine Weir, 21st February 1956.
[258] Roberts, *Edward Cooney*, 33.
[259] Roberts, *Cooney*, 33.

Since the 'selective fulfilment of Matthew 10' would logically follow 'the nature of the mission', it will be appropriate to consider that before 'the basis for the homeless, unsalaried worker'.

The Nature Of The Mission

The instructions in Matthew 10 are very explicit, 'Go not into the way of the Gentiles, and any city of the Samaritans enter ye not. But go rather to the lost sheep of the house of Israel'. France explains the significance of this instruction at this time in Jesus' ministry:

> *Rather this saying reflects the historic fact that with few exceptions (8:5-13 deals with a Gentile in Jewish territory; 15:21-28 is clearly presented as exceptional) the mission of both Jesus and his disciples before the resurrection was in fact limited to Israel; the time for the Gentile mission was later. The emphasis of the saying lies not primarily on the prohibition of a wider mission, but on the priority of the mission to Israel. To call Israel to repentance was the primary focus of Jesus' ministry; the call was urgent and demanded total concentration (cf. 10:23).[260]*

It would be remiss of any study to consider the sending of the twelve apostles as recorded in Matthew 10: 5-15 in isolation from the parallel passages of Mark 6:7-13 and Luke 9: 1-5. If these instructions were so vitally important in that they were to serve as permanent model of ministry for all time it is reasonable to expect them to mirror each other. There is a considerable variation in requirements between Mark's account and those of Matthew and Luke. Mark permits taking a staff while it is forbidden in Matthew and Luke; Mark permits sandals while footwear is forbidden in Matthew.

The 2x2 workers refuse to recognise any disparity in the accounts so can they be reconciled without considering as some scholars do that these differences point to an errancy of Scripture? Blomberg points out, 'all three Gospels agree on the basic concept of travelling light;

---

[260] France, R.T, *Matthew*, (Leicester: Inter-Varsity Press, 1985), 178.

only the details differ – but this solution must still admit the presence of a contradiction, even if it is coincidental.'[261] To support the inerrancy of Scripture various solutions have been offered but some of these only exacerbate the problem by raising new problems. According to Blomberg, 'a source-critical solution does seem preferable – but with some distinct nuances offered by Osborne.'[262] The reconstruction offered is:

> *Luke 10: 1-12 describes Jesus' subsequent sending of the seventy, which contains closer parallels to Matthew 9:37 – 10:16 than does Luke 9:1-6. Matthew has consequently conflated Mark's account of the sending of the twelve with Luke's account of the seventy . . . while Luke has assimilated some material from chapter 10 of his account in Chapter nine. In other words the prohibition against staff and sandals originally stemmed only from the latter mission; in the former Jesus did permit these two items. Is this reconstruction compatible with the doctrine of inerrancy? Indiscriminate conflation and assimilation certainly is not, but in this case Osborne's solution works precisely because the twelve were most likely part of the seventy. . . Matthew and Luke each presents (sic) entirely factual reports of what Jesus told his disciples before sending them out to minister in His name, even if they do not spell out the number and nature of these missions as clearly as the modern readers might have wished.[263]*

Jesus did send his apostles/disciples on a mission and in the final analysis, there is no level of disagreement between the three accounts that would give rise to controversy as to their historicity.

An important lesson to learn from this is that, given the nature of the mission, there is simply no way from Matthew 10 or the passages of Mark and Luke that this can be interpreted as the only foundation for ministry in the future. There is further evidence that is not the only foundation from reading of the diversity of ministers and workers for the spread of the Gospel in Acts and throughout the remainder of the New Testament.

---

[261] Blomberg, Craig L, 'The Legitimacy and Limits of Harmonization' in Carson, D. A and Woodbridge, John D, editors, *Hermeneutics, Authority and Canon*, (Grand Rapids: Baker Books, 1985), 154.

[262] Blomberg is citing Osborne's work, *Evangelical and Redaction Criticism.*

[263] Blomberg, 'The Legitimacy and Limits of Harmonization', 155.

Selective Fulfilment Of Matthew 10

Other important aspects of the mission in Matthew 10 that conflict with 2x2 practices is there is no reference to the sending out of women on the mission. This observation is not against the principle of women in ministry but simply making the point that literal adherence to Matthew 10 excludes women from the 2x2 ministry. Indications are that the majority of 2x2 workers are currently women.[264] So how do the 2x2 workers interpret this? One Overseer responded, 'In Acts 2, the Holy Spirit made it clear that women have the same spiritual inspiration as men and have a right to express it. It took time for some doctrines (for example Jesus' command to go to the Gentiles) to be fully realized.'[265]

Matthew 10:8 is the most difficult part of the mission for the 2x2s to reconcile with their present ministry. The commands to the twelve apostles were clear and explicit: heal the sick, cleanse the lepers, raise the dead, cast out devils. Workers ignore this command. I asked a 2x2 overseer how they interpreted this verse and he responded, 'this chapter is explicitly for the 12 first apostles. Luke 10 gives similar instructions to the 70. Of course, all 82 were sent to Jews only and seemingly for a limited mission. However, we read about apostles in Acts and the letters and observe that they kept to many of the same principles, although perhaps not in every detail.'[266] A senior Irish worker commented on Matthew 10:8:

> Because Jesus was sending them to the Jews this is why the healings were so important. This was related to the promise to the Jewish people that if they did God's will none of the diseases would come upon them. If we go back to the Old Testament this was a promise given to the children of Israel and not given to the Gentiles. That is why healings are not relevant to our ministry today'.[267]

---

[264] In July 2011 the breakdown of workers in Ireland and the United Kingdom was 65 women and 46 men. Source: Email 7th July 2011.

[265] Email 16th January 2012.

[266] Email 16th January 2012.

[267] Meeting with workers 20th January 2012.

Commenting on the movement's selectivity in advocating parts of Matthew 10 as their model of ministry, Craig Blomberg stated, 'They cannot pick and choose the parts of this passage that suits them. By claiming that they are following the path of this mission commanded then they must incorporate every aspect between verses five and fourteen.'[268]

The homeless, unsalaried minister

Referring to the task in Mark which is the only account that mentions a two and two ministry, Cole posits, 'this task demanded a scattering of personnel, a wandering ministry, and a deliberate renunciation, a studied simplicity of lifestyle, designed both to encourage and demonstrate trust in God.'[269] As we read all three accounts are we to deduce from these that Christian ministers are to live homeless and unsalaried as they preach the Gospel? For this mission only it was Jesus' command that his disciples take along no money or provision for their itinerant preaching but to rely solely on the generosity of those to whom they minister. The homeless and penniless preacher is emphasised in the 2x2 preaching and at times they manage to find support for their ministry in texts that simply have nothing remotely to do with the ministry. An example of such preaching is by one worker, David Delaney. Following a reading from Nehemiah, he proceeded to preach as follows:

> *In that third chapter [Nehemiah 3:3] there is the fish gate and I don't know but the thought came into my mind that the fish gate of what Jesus said when he called Peter James and John and the other disciples and he called them from their occupations, from their professions and their jobs and he said I will make you fishers of men. He was going to send them out to become fishers of men and we are very thankful that this ministry that Jesus established when*

---

[268] Discussion with Craig Blomberg in Dublin 11th January 2012. Blomberg is Distinguished Professor of New Testament, Denver Seminary, Colorado.
[269] Cole, R. Alan, *Mark*, 2nd edition, (Leicester: Inter-Varsity Press, 1989), 86.

he was on the earth that this has not changed... And you know that is what Jesus [said] when he sent them into the world, was to go into the world having left everything, their occupations, their families, their jobs, everything that was near and dear, everything that was important. When he said to his apostles, he told them to leave everything and we are thankful that this example of the fish gate has never changed. It is still the same, the same and we have the faith to believe that it still works and that it still happens and it is still in the Bible and his word today because God ordained it and God set it in order.[270]

It is difficult to understand how a reading of this text can lead to this pattern of thought but it does show how extraordinarily poor 2x2 workers are at exegesis when they interpret the 'fish gate' of Nehemiah as support for the 2x2 ministry.

The use of Matthew 10 as support for a homeless, unsalaried ministry indicates that Irvine, Cooney their fellow workers and those since are quite prepared to simply take texts of Scripture and misapply them. Their first converts believed their interpretation of Matthew 10 and this is still prevalent today. While the 2x2s hold to a literal interpretation of parts of Matthew 10: 5-15 they patently ignore other parts of this text such as Matthew 10:10b, 'for the workman is worthy of his meat.' According to Strong's Concordance the Greek word for meat used here is, '*trophe* – by implications rations (wages): - food, meat.'[271] It is therefore reasonable to conclude that even at this stage in the mission Jesus shows concern that the apostles will have adequate provision. In Luke's account of the sending of the seventy, and the instructions are similar to the sending of the twelve, we find the statement in Luke 10:7, 'For the labourer is worthy of his hire.' It is interesting that the Greek word used is *misthos* and according to Strong's Concordance this means, 'apparently a primary word: pay for service (literal or figurative), good or bad: - hire, reward, wages.'[272] Here the apostles are to rely on the generosity of those to whom they minister.

---

[270] Fermanagh convention, Saturday morning, June 2011.

[271] Baker Warren, editor, *Strong's Complete Word Study Concordance*, (Chattanooga: AMG Publishers, 2004), 5157.

[272] Baker, *Strong's Complete Word Study Concordance*, 3408.

There is a change or a reversal of this practice by Jesus in Luke 22: 35 and 36: 'And he said to them, When I sent you without purse and scrip, and shoes, lacked ye any thing? And they said, Nothing. Then he said to them, But now, he that hath a purse, let him take it and likewise his scrip'. Not only did Jesus change an earlier command but according to Klein, Blomberg and Hubbard, 'Paul does this, too, changing or reversing earlier practices later on in his ministry. . . The rationale in each case is what most effectively advances the cause of the gospel (1 Cor 9).'[273] In 1 Corinthians 9: 9 – 10 Paul writes, 'For it is written in the law of Moses, Thou shalt not muzzle the ox that treadeth out the corn. Doth God take care of the oxen? Or saith he it altogether for our sakes? For our sakes, no doubt this is written: that he that ploweth should plow in hope; and that he that thresheth in hope should be partaker of his hope.' Commenting on the meaning of these verses Blomberg says, 'pay your pastors generously.'[274] This is a significant text that supports a paid ministry.

Paul reiterates this instruction for the church when writing to Timothy, "For the Scripture says, you shall not muzzle the ox that treads out the grain, and, The labourer deserves his wages" (1 Timothy 5:18). The same Greek word, *misthos* that is translated here as 'wages' or 'reward' is translated 'hire' in Luke 10:7, 'for the labourer is worthy of his hire'. Here Paul was referring very specifically to those preaching and teaching. Writing to the Corinthian church in support of Barnabas and himself, Paul uses the same Old Testament text but with more weight: "For it is written in the Law of Moses, 'You shall not muzzle an ox when it treads out the grain,' Is it for the oxen that God is concerned? Does he not speak entirely for our sake?"(1 Corinthians 9:9-10a ESV). Instone-Brewer posits that: 'In this exegesis, Paul has derived from the law the right of a Christian worker to wages. He has based this on a literal interpretation of Deuteronomy 25:4 and on the contemporary understanding of the term "ox" in the law as a reference to all types of labourer, human and animal.'[275] This view finds support from many

[273] Klein, William W, Blomberg, Craig L and Hubbard, Robert L, *Introduction to Biblical Interpretation*, (Nashville: Thomas Nelson, 1993), 489.
[274] Blomberg's lecture on biblical interpretation during an MA module in Dublin, 11th January 2012.
[275] Instone-Brewer, David, 'Paul's Literal Interpretation of "Do Not Muzzle the Ox"' in Helm, Paul and Trueman, Carl, editors, *The Trustworthiness of God*, (Leicester: Apollos, 2002), 147.

leading scholars and Sanders develops this theme in more detail when he writes:

> *The principal reservation that must stand over this entire discussion is that Paul as a rule does not cite commandments – either those in the law, those "from the Lord," or those of his own making – and then say they should be obeyed. There are only a few instances in which the motive or rationale behind an instruction is said to be that God commanded it. . . He regards Deut. 25:24 as the Lord's command that "those who proclaim the gospel should get their living from the gospel" (1 Cor. 9:8f., 14).[276]*

Many scholars have studied and commented upon this particular application by Paul. Moo posits, 'here Paul appears to equate the "literal" sense with the "spiritual," Christian sense.'[277] It is important to consider how Paul arrived at the decision that this Old Testament principle had an important application since this has major significance for this study. Paul's use and application of this Old Testament passage is described by Instone-Brewer, 'it is unique because it is the time when Paul derives a new law from the Scripture. New laws, or *halakot*, are very common in rabbinic Judaism but this is the only occasion we see it in the writings of Paul.'[278] Moo points out, 'What Paul does is to draw out in a legitimate way the significance of the law for the situation of churches and their "workers".'[279]

Because of the widely accepted principle of the right of Christian workers to have generous support from the churches in which they labour, and because this principle is an antithesis to 2x2s' model of ministry, it is important to take space to consider Paul's exegesis fully. Instone-Brewer expands on this when he writes:

276   Sanders, E. P, *Paul, the Law and the Jewish People,* (London: SCM Press, 1985), 107.
277   Moo, Douglas J, 'The Problem of Sensus Plenior' in Carson, D. A. and Woodridge, John D, editors, *Hermeneutics, Authority and Canon,* (Grand Rapids: Baker Books, 1986), 189.
278   Instone-Brewer, 'Paul's Literal Interpretation', 152-153.
279   Moo, Problem of Sensus Plenior, 189.

In 1 Corinthians 9:9-11, Paul cites his text and then presents an exegesis in four stages: In the Law of Moses it is written: "You shall not muzzle a threshing ox."

1. Is God concerned with oxen? [No]

2. Is it not surely/altogether (*pantos*) said for us? [Yes]

3. Certainly it was written for us because: He who ploughs should plough in hope, and he who treshes (sic) [should tresh] in hope that he will partake.

4. If we sowed spiritual things for you, much more should we reap material things from you.

Paul used the timeless technique of arguing from what is accepted towards that which he wished to prove. Stages 1-3 all have parallels in rabbinic legislation and would be met with approval. Point four is the conclusion when these are accepted.[280]

When I asked a 2x2 overseer to comment on these Scriptures, it is obvious from the reply that they choose to ignore Paul's exegesis. Referring back to Matthew 10: 5-15 I asked, 'As far as the purse and scrip is concerned it appears that this condition was rescinded by Jesus in Luke 22:35-36. How do the workers interpret this?' The response I received was, 'I don't split hairs on those points and from what we read about Paul's missions, he didn't either, but he kept to the main principles of not soliciting money from those he preached to and taking a companion with him whenever possible. We have proven this to be sound doctrine when put into practice.'[281]

I needed some clarity on his response and I then asked, 'It is not a case of splitting hairs here but Jesus' earlier command of Matthew 10:9-10 was changed in Luke 22:35-36 coupled with Paul's injunction in 1 Cor 9:9-11 and 1Tim 5:18 – 'Thou shall not muzzle the ox, etc'. there

---

[280] Instone-Brewer, Paul's Literal Interpretation, 143-144.
[281] Email 16th January 2012.

seems to be a case for a much more open and transparent financial support for ministers of the gospel?' His response was, 'The other points you mention aren't worth arguing about . . . and I hope that doesn't offend you. I have my convictions, but don't try to force them on anyone else.' [282]

This overseer's response is typical of the approach the 2x2s take when faced with an exegesis that in any way undermines their model of ministry. Instone-Brewer's conclusion, 'Paul has derived from the law the right of Christian workers to wages.'[283] will not be countenanced by the 2x2 movement. Based on Paul's exegesis one can only conclude that the statements made by Cooney were completely unsubstantiated by any intelligent interpretation of Scripture.

In the early part of the 20th century, the experience of the clergy in established churches was not one where they enjoyed a high standard of living. In a statement made to the general Synod of the Church of Ireland in 1920 by Primate D'Arcy, he refers to the heavy workload and low incomes of the clergy. D'Arcy called for a regrouping of parishes and the provision of adequate remuneration. According to D'Arcy the present system was, 'subjecting many clergy to the grinding tyranny of abject poverty. . . [the clergy need] not only a living wage, but a man's work.'[284] Here is a picture of poorly paid and overworked clergy that hardly reflects Cooney's denunciation of the clergy in no uncertain terms.[285] Although today's 2x2s disown Cooney, much of what he said and taught is current in their own teaching today. Certainly, the 2x2s oppose any form of a paid ministry and see this as unscriptural.

---

[282] Email 20th January 2012
[283] Instone-Brewer, Paul's Literal Interpretation, 147.
[284] Acheson, Alan, *A History of the Church of Ireland 1691 – 2001*, 2nd Edition, (Dublin: Columba Press, 2002), 219
[285] Roberts, *Cooney*, 67.

The Mission Of God

The mission of God and the mission of Jesus Christ are inextricably bound together so by examining the mission of God what emerges is the entire picture of the mission of Jesus as recorded in the New Testament. Stott explains:

> The essence of evangelical faith is that in Jesus Christ incarnate, crucified, raised and exalted, God has spoken and acted decisively and finally for the salvation of the world. In consequence, Jesus Christ is God's last word to the world; it is inconceivable that there should be any higher revelation than what he has given in his Son.[286]

After four hundred years between Malachi and Matthew the silence was broken by the birth, as prophesied, of Jesus in Bethlehem. In Jesus Christ there is the fulfillment of the mission of God, the story of redemption that was first promised in Genesis 3:15. The prologue to John's Gospel has a rich description of the incarnation (John 1:1-18). The dominant theme is that after the long silence, God speaks. He makes himself known to man through the Word. 'And the Word became flesh and dwelt among us, and we have seen his glory, glory as of the only Son from the Father, full of grace and truth' (John 1:14). Stott comments, 'that is why the hallmark of evangelicalism is an insistence on *sola scriptura* and *sola gratia*. They arise from *solus Chritus: Christ alone for revelation and redemption.'*[287]

In 2x2 preaching there is an absence of the importance of the person and work of Christ. Their preaching exhorts their members to follow the example of Jesus. It is therefore appropriate to contrast the actions of the workers with the earthly ministry of Jesus. The workers see themselves as direct descendants of and performing the same role as the early apostles[288] appointed by Jesus. Have the workers any parallels with the appointment and role of the twelve apostles? The apostles were men from various walks of life. It is evident from Scripture that

---

[286] Stott, *Living Church*, 173.
[287] Stott, *Living Church*, 173.
[288] Confirmed by Tommie Gamble, the Overseer for Ireland in a discussion on 13th February 2012.

some were married, owned their homes[289] and had families. Workers are unmarried,[290] homeless and without possessions. Workers believe that they replicate the ministry of Jesus. Leeper preached:

> *To believe in Jesus we must also follow the example that he was and believe in the ministry that he established himself. We need to find a ministry [2x2 workers] with the same spirit that Jesus had. For someone to receive salvation they need to come into contact with that ministry. The ministry that has the same spirit that Jesus had when he was on this earth. And that is a vital part of salvation.[291]*

This is typical of 2x2 preaching where the emphasis is on the ministry as 'a vital part of salvation.' The four Gospels leave a clear picture of Jesus' earthly ministry and while they are all broadly similar there are differences; however, these are not significantly different to cause any doctrinal problems. Packer writes, 'they were composed at a time when Jesus was still remembered, and misstatements about him could be identified. They were accepted were accepted everywhere, it seems, as soon as they were known, though the early Christians as a body were not credulous and detected spurious gospels with skill.'[292] The Gospels present Jesus as a man of many sides who mixed freely with publicans and sinners, called the twelve to participate in His mission, taught in the temple and the synagogues, performed miracles, confronted the Pharisees and other Jews, attended a wedding, shared table fellowship with a Pharisee and eventually completed His mission by dying on a cross, followed by the resurrection and ascension. It is erroneous to lift a few verses from the Gospels and treat these as detailing the most important aspects of the mission of Jesus. The sending out of the twelve in Matthew 10 and the seventy in Luke 10 were important aspects of the mission of Jesus. His life and his ministry were but a prologue for the main event that encompassed his death, resurrection and ascension. Close study of the Synoptic Gospels and John's Gospel shows that whatever situation Jesus was in and especially in the company of publicans and sinners he was always conscious that He had a mission to fulfill.

---

[289] The homeless preacher is an important distinctive of the 2x2 ministry.
[290] A condition of the ministry although many of the early workers were married.
[291] Andrew Leeper. Bleary mission 9th February 2012.
[292] Packer, J. I, *Truth and Power*, (Guildford: Eagle Publishing, 1996), 31.

Throughout His earthly ministry, despite claims to the contrary, Jesus did not leave a model for ministry or church government. Stott writes, 'on the contrary, the Church is God's new community. For his purpose, conceived in a past eternity, being worked out in history, and to be perfected in a future eternity, is not just to save isolated individuals and to perpetuate our loneliness, but rather to build his church, to call out of the world a people for his own glory.'[293] In each of the four Gospels there are different emphases as to what each writer considered important in church and ministry. All four Gospels are of equal importance but this study will concentrate on Luke's account of the ministry of Jesus.

Luke's Gospel has the most detailed accounts that portray the compassion of Jesus Christ and his ready response to those in need. Luke, sometimes seen as the outsider, starts off by telling us why he has written an account: 'Inasmuch as many have undertaken to complete a narrative of the things that have been accomplished . . . that you may have certainty concerning the things you were taught' (Luke 1:1-4).

Here is no secondhand account of the story of Jesus but one that is validated by those who were there from the beginning. Luke's Gospel is the longest of the four and by adding his authorship of Acts he is the largest single contributor to the New Testament. What strikes most readers of Luke's Gospel is how Jesus' humanity shines through, particularly in his association with and compassion for numerous categories of social outcasts. According to Blomberg, 'Four groups stand out in particular. (1) Samaritans and Gentiles; (2) tax collectors; (3) women and (4) the poor.'[294] Luke's presentation of Jesus as Saviour, an important motif in this Gospel, fits the view of the compassionate and caring Jesus. Among the groups who benefit from Jesus' compassion are those whom Morris labels, 'the disreputable.'[295]

McMahan identifies five common characteristics of what he calls 'type-scenes of meals with outcasts' involving Jesus in the Gospel of Luke:

---

[293] Stott, *Living Church*, 19-20.
[294] Blomberg, Craig L, *Jesus and the Gospels*, (Leicester: Apollos, 1997), 145.
[295] Morris, Leon, *Luke*, (Nottingham: Inter-Varsity Press, 1988), 51.

1. Jesus or his representatives eat with those who in some sense are considered second-class citizens in Israel.

2. These outcasts regularly respond to Jesus' message with joy.

3. Pharisees and Scribes, by way of contrast, equally commonly grumble and complain about Jesus' behaviour.

4. The episodes are consistently introduced by calls to discipleship.

5. Finally, the scenes regularly conclude with a statement of Jesus' mission and redemptive purpose in order to refute the objections raised against his behaviour.[296]

The Jesus of the Gospels never lost sight of His mission and used every opportunity to reach out to those whom he saw as the lost, the poor and the needy. He was by no means an isolationist who took the view that those to whom he reached out had to come to the Temple or the synagogue. Jesus met them at the point of their need and did not burden them with preconditions as to his acceptance of them. There were the actions of Jesus that can be interpreted as radical such as praising the faith of pagans and urging Jews to learn from their example. McDermott writes:

> *He commended the widow of Zarephath and Naaman when visiting Nazareth (Luke 4:14-30). Both were pagans who put their faith in the word of a Hebrew prophet. Jesus was "amazed" by the faith of the centurion who sought healing for his slave, observing that he had not seen such faith among the Jews (Luke 7:9). Jesus also lauded the faith of the Canaanite woman in Matthew 15, recommended the ethical behavior of the Good Samaritan, and pointed out that a "foreigner" was the only leper among the ten to "return and give praise to God" (Luke 17:18 NIV). In all three cases Jesus applauded the acts of faith of people who were not yet inside the Jewish or Christian circles of faith and he recommended that his hearers learn from their examples.[297]*

---

[296] McMahan Craig cited by Blomberg, *Contagious Holiness*, 130.

[297] McDermott, Gerald R, 'What if Paul had been from China?' in Stackhouse, John G, Editor, *No other Gods before Me*, (Grand Rapids: Baker Academic, 2001), 20.

Contrast the scenes in Luke's Gospel with those attending a 2x2 mission or convention (although some other Christian movements differ little), with men dressed in suits and women suitably attired in long skirts or dresses with long hair up in a bun; it would be difficult for an outsider and especially one that would be poorly attired to feel at ease in such company. In my attendance at missions and conventions I have yet to see anyone who does not meet the unwritten dress code. Commenting on Luke's Gospel, Blomberg says, 'Luke 19:10 arguably provides a one-verse summary of the entire Gospel: "For the Son of Man came to seek and to save what was lost".'[298]

The 2x2 ministry stands in stark contrast to the examples used by McMahan and McDermott. In their sermons the workers constantly point to Jesus as their example,[299] yet they have little or no interaction or contact with those outside the movement. As I have observed the lifestyle of various workers, they are cosseted from the real world in that they spend their entire lives residing in the homes of members and rarely interact with anyone outside the movement. With their emphasis on Jesus as their example they could reasonably be expected to demonstrate and repeat some examples of his behaviour found in the Gospels. In Luke's gospel Jesus is either going to a meal, at a meal or coming from a meal. In addressing the Pharisees of his day Jesus stated, 'the Son of man is coming eating and drinking; and ye say, behold a gluttonous man and a winebibber, a friend of publicans and sinners' (Luke 7:34).

Chester comments, 'Jesus spent his time eating and drinking - a lot of his time. His mission strategy was a long meal, stretching into the evening. He did evangelism and discipleship round a table with some grilled fish, a load of bread and a jug of wine.'[300] Such a statement in the eyes of the 2x2s would be greeted with dismay and looked upon as highly irreverent. It is only if the gospels are read with a preconceived idea as to how Jesus should be viewed that one misses the humanity of Jesus as shown in so many situations. There are many examples in the Gospels and in Luke in particular where Jesus showed his compassion.

---

[298] Blomberg, *Jesus and the Gospels*, 146.
[299] The theme of Jesus as the example will be considered under the heading of conversion.
[300] Chester, Tim, *A Meal with Jesus*, (Nottingham: Inter-Varsity Press, 2011), 13.

An excellent demonstration of the pragmatism of Jesus is recorded in Luke 19: 1-10 where there is a record of his encounter with Zacchaeus. There are several important aspects of this account and these are summarized by Bailey:

1. Jesus offers costly love to Zacchaeus.

2. Zacchaeus accepts that love and in so doing accepts being found. That acceptance is his *repentance*, which takes place as he descends from the tree to welcome Jesus to his house.

3. Zacchaeus is given the huge gift of acceptance in the eyes of Jesus. Jesus is willing to enter his house and eat his "polluted" food and sleep in his "defiled" guest bed.

4. Zacchaeus responds to Jesus' gift out of the deepest level of who he (Zacchaeus) is, and the model of his response is what Jesus has done for him. Zacchaeus receives costly love and is thereby empowered and motivated to offer costly love to others. His engagement in mission has already begun.[301]

From the workers' insistence on using Jesus as their example 2x2 workers, and indeed others who are involved in mission, must learn that in his ministry Jesus operated outside the norms expected from him. Workers will tell how they go into areas and hold missions and as I write this they are holding one in my district, less than a mile from my home. Their idea of outreach is by dropping a little card through the doors in the district inviting people to come and 'listen to the story of Jesus as it is recorded in John's Gospel.'[302] This is a far cry from the ministry of Jesus and the apostles which was constantly on the move and interacted with those most in need. Blomberg summarizes the Zacchaeus account in these words:

Jesus so cares for those rightly or wrongly stigmatized by society that

---

[301] Bailey, Kenneth E, *Jesus Through Middle Eastern Eyes*, (London: SPCK, 2008), 182.
[302] 2x2 mission commenced on Thursday 19th January 2012 and was held every Thursday night in the Young Farmers Hall, Bleary, County Armagh, Northern Ireland.

he ignores conventional restrictions on intimately associating with them. He is willing to go to their homes. Indeed, here he insists on it. He shares their food and lodging, but he never does it simply for inclusiveness' sake. A call to repentance is always implicit unless, as here, the individual in question takes the initiative to declare his change of heart and behavior.[303]

The outcome of Jesus reaching out to Zacchaeus demonstrates the effectiveness of a ministry that is not so bound up with rules that it fails to minister to those treated as outcasts by society. Bailey points out:

Jesus observes hostility against Zacchaeus and transfers it to himself. . . By entering Zacchaeus's house for the night, Jesus grants Zacchaeus the gift of a new status, that of acceptance in Jesus' sight. . . Jesus declares that "Salvation has come" to the house of Zacchaeus before Zacchaeus carries out the restitution he promises. Salvation is clearly more than a single decision, it is also a process that affects all of life. Jesus is the agent of that salvation, and he is the one that brings salvation to Zacchaeus's house. . . In his inauguration Jesus declares his ministry to involve proclamation, justice advocacy and compassion (Luke 4: 16-30). All three elements are present in this story.[304]

In discussion with a senior Irish worker I referred to the example of believers after Pentecost and suggested that in the New Testament there is no category for a silent witness and that believers are called to be witnesses. He pointed out that when workers arrive in an area they depend upon the friends [members] to be the link with the people that they never meet. He pointed to folk at work and school who do not say anything about their faith and yet outsiders see 'this person has something I haven't got'. They ask questions and then the opportunity arises to invite them into a gospel meeting. 'We don't go around publicly trying to push something down people's throats', he stated.

It is not a case of going along asking someone if they are a Christian but quietly living in front of them in the everyday things of life so they depend on the friends to show the example. He talked of people coming to the meetings because of the examples they had seen in

----

[303] Blomberg, Craig L, *Contagious Holiness*, (Downers Grove: Apollos, 2005), 156.
[304] Bailey, *Jesus Through Middle Eastern Eyes*, 184-185.

someone's life. 'That is the witness we like to hear about.'[305]

I pointed out that I observed that the New Testament Christians were more proactive in their witnessing when we see how quickly the gospel spread compared to the 2x2 movement. He said this was a special time and there have been other special times. I suggested that this must be a special time, given the billions who are lost and never heard of Christ. He replied that their whole work is depending upon the Spirit to guide.[306] The claim that they depend upon the Spirit to guide must be respected but where the guidance is at variance with the commands we find in Scripture then it is important to point out that Scripture validates experience and not vice versa. The New Testament believers were called upon to be witnesses and that cannot be interpreted passively. Stott writes:

> *What impels the Christian to be active in witness? The basic motive is plain obedience. Every Christian is a servant of Christ. He has been 'bought with a price' and is now attached to his master by bonds of grateful obedience. 'The love of Christ controls us.' It has us in a grip. Indeed, since our new life is due entirely to Christ's death, His love hems us in and 'leaves us no choice' but to live for Him. In seeking to live for Christ we are concerned to do his will and to keep His commandments, all of them. We are not at liberty to pick and choose. Nor do we wish to. So we do not overlook His commandment, to 'go . . . and make disciples.'[307]*

When it comes to witnessing to their faith there is an inertia amongst 2x2 members and workers that is completely at variance with the enthusiastic dissemination of the message of Jesus Christ by the first-century believers; that to them was an act of obedience.

Moving from Luke's Gospel to Luke's account of the early church in the Acts of the Apostles the movement is transformed by Pentecost. In the first chapter of Acts it is recorded that Jesus expected his followers to be, 'my witnesses in Jerusalem and in all Judea and Samaria, and to the end of the earth' (Acts 1:8). Peter's sermon on the Day of

---

[305] Senior worker, 20th January 2012.
[306] Discussion with two workers on 20th January 2012.
[307] Stott, John, *Our Guilty Silence*, (Leicester: Inter-Varsity Press, 1967), 18.

Pentecost and subsequent sermons recorded in Acts must be examples for preachers. From his exposition of Old Testament Scriptures he preached the Gospel emphasizing the significance of the death and resurrection of Christ. For Peter it was important to extol the Lordship of Christ (Acts 2:36) and the result was startling. Unlike what sometimes happens at the end of a 2x2 mission where an opportunity is given for those who want to profess, to indicate this by standing, the listeners cry out, 'men and brethren, what shall we do?' Then there is Peter's call to repentance and Scripture teaches that this is the first step on the road to faith in Christ. In Mark's Gospel Jesus' message was, 'repent ye, and believe the gospel' (1:15). There are many examples of workers' sermons published on the internet and I have transcripts of those that I have heard preached at conventions and missions, and there is a stark contrast between the content of these sermons and what was preached to the listeners in the Acts of the Apostles.

I agree with Daniel when he writes, 'the "Workers" themselves tend to speak only in vague platitudes and analogies. Most of what is said is couched in orthodox-sounding terminology.'[308] On close analysis they never exegete the passage of Scripture from which they read and apart from a few general comments of little consequence they never get anywhere close to having an application of the message to the listeners. An example of such preaching is when the worker read from Romans 10:1-8 and after speaking in general terms for around fifteen minutes finished off this sermon:

> *You know this really is very touching because this chapter is also speaking to us about faith that comes by hearing which is what has been put there very nicely. He said the faith, that faith…. But the righteousness which is of faith speaketh on this wise, say not in thine heart, Who shall ascend into heaven? to bring God down, or, say not in thine heart, who shall descend into the deep? to bring Christ down. That's not our salvation, that's not how faith comes, that's not how faith comes. Even if we did have the ability to bring Christ down and to bring Christ up so to speak, even in our own abilities and our own powers that's not going to, that's not faith, that's not how faith*

---

[308] Daniel, *Reinventing the Truth*, 19.

comes. Faith comes by hearing and hearing by the Word of God, hearing the Word of God, imagine that's how faith comes. The rich man, the rich man in Lazarus, the rich man when he awakens and found that he was in the horrors of hell. It was an awful experience for that man. But I believe that God in His mercy in the chapter in Luke, he gave us, he drew back the curtain so to speak and gives us a picture of what it would be like to finish up in hell. You know… that man was so concerned, he realized he was there, he didn't want to be there. A terrible experience the rich man. And there he was in torment, he wanted someone to come along and dip his finger in water and cool his tongue. He said I'm tormented in this flame. And then he said this, he said I have five brethren, he talked to Lazarus. And he said I have five brethren and he says I don't want them to come to this torment. He didn't want them to be there either. But anyway, then he said if someone had risen from the dead and go back and speak to them that would believe, that they would believe, that's what he said. No the Lord said no even though someone did rise from the dead it wouldn't make any difference, they still won't believe. He says they still won't believe. That's not how faith comes, someone rising from the dead. It would be miraculous but that's not how faith comes, faith comes from hearing and hearing by the word of Christ. It's a beautiful picture to see how faith comes and without faith it is impossible to please God.[309]

It is difficult to surmise how a preacher can navigate through the passage of Romans 10: 1-8 and end his sermon in this way. Such preaching lacks the focus on the main theme of the Gospel of Jesus Christ. After listening to several 2x2 sermons over the past three years, the words of Photius, the Patriarch when describing the Apostolic Father, Clement, come to mind, 'the ideas are somewhat scattered and do not maintain a coherent continuity.'[310]

....

[309] Sermon preached by Herbie Jennings in Corcrain, 25th October 2010.
[310] Parvis, Paul, '2 Clement and the Meaning of the Christian Homily' in Foster, Paul, editor, *The Writings of the Apostolic Fathers*, (London: T&T Clark, 2007), 32.

Throughout this study I have had the opportunity to see the movement at close quarters and there is little evidence that they resemble the New Testament church of Acts 2:42-47. Commenting on the marks of the church in this passage Stott says:

> Looking back over these marks of the first Spirit-filled community, it is evident that they all concerned the church's relationships. First, they were related to the apostles (in submission). They were eager to receive the apostles' instruction . . . Secondly, they related to each other (in love). They persevered in fellowship, supporting each other and caring for the needs of the poor. . . Thirdly, they were related to God (in worship). They worshipped him in the temple and in the home, in the Lord's Supper and in the prayers, with joy and with reverence. . . Fourthly, they related to the world (in outreach). They were engaged in continuous evangelism. No self-centred (sic). Self-contained church (absorbed in its own parochial affairs) can claim to be filled with the Spirit. So a Spirit-filled church is a missionary church.[311]

There is little in the 2x2 movement that corresponds with Stott's description of the church in Acts. Since the local church is a community of regenerated believers, it must be guided by Scripture and in Acts 2:38 there is Peter's very distinctive call to repentance followed by baptism for the forgiveness of sins. In response to the word the listeners are baptized, 'and there were added that day about three thousand souls' (Acts 2:41). Stott points out:

> He [Jesus Christ] did not add them to the church without saving them (no nominal Christianity at the beginning) nor did he save them without adding them to the church (no solitary Christianity either). Salvation and church membership belong together; they still do.[312]

It is evident from this passage and later references in Acts that the apostles were in leadership and teaching roles. Here was a community of believers who devoted themselves to the apostles' teaching and in fellowship together breaking bread and praying (Acts 2:38).

....
[311] Stott, John R. W, *The Message of Acts*, 2nd edition (Leicester: IVP, 1991), 87.
[312] Stott, *Acts*, 87.

As the Church moved from the New Testament into the immediate post-apostolic age the extant writings from this period are by no means numerous but they are sufficient to demonstrate how the early church progressed following the death of the apostles. The 2x2 workers see themselves as following in succession to the twelve apostles but there is no evidence to support that leadership of the early church believed this, as Bray explains:

> *The second-generation leadership – Clement, Ignatius and others – continued in the apostolic style to some extent, but they never claimed, nor were they given, apostolic authority. . . From the age of revelation the Church was passing to the age of defence and confirmation of the gospel – a new situation demanding new skills and attitudes, but one which in terms of faith and doctrine the Church aimed to remain in the strictest continuity with apostolic times.[313]*

There was a hierarchy in the early church and it is evident that Clement was Bishop of Rome but that status did not confer upon him any special authority over other Churches. His writing to the Church of Corinth was not on matters of doctrine but of behaviour where the young men in the Church were trying to usurp power. In c. AD100 Clement exhorted the Church in Corinth:

> *The apostles received the gospel for our sakes from the Lord Jesus Christ; Jesus Christ was sent from God. The Christ therefore is from God and the apostles from the Christ. . . So preaching in the country and city, they appointed their firstfruits, having tested them by the Spirit, to be bishops and deacons of those who should believe . . . Our apostles also knew through our Lord Jesus Christ that there would be strife over the name of the bishop's office. . . Men, therefore, who were appointed by the apostles, or subsequently by other eminent men, with the approval of the whole Church, and have ministered blamelessly to the flock of Christ . . . such men are unjustly deposed of their ministry.[314]*

Clement was close to the source and his writings indicate that the first

---

[313] Bray, Gerald, *Creeds, Councils and Christ*, (Leicester: Inter-Varsity Press, 1984), 48-49.
[314] Stevenson, J. Revised by Frend, W.H.C, *A New Eusebius*, revised edition, (London: SPCK, 1987), 8-9.

and early second-century church had a structure that was put in place by the first apostles. Importantly the appointment of a bishop was not the role of the few but of the whole Church. Highlighting the importance of the role of the bishop in the early Church, Frend writes, 'in the seven genuine letters of Ignatius the word *episcopos* (*episcopein*) occurs no less than fifty-five times.'[315]

From the writings of the early church fathers there are no references to the style of ministry we find in the 2x2 movement. In the second-century church the role of the apologist was beginning to emerge and this was essential to combat the Gnostic heresies and the teachings of Marcion. 'Marcion believed that Jesus and the God of the OT were opposites, and anything in Christian writings that smacked of Judaism ought to be expunged.'[316] In the middle of that century Justin Martyr who had a background in Stoic and Platonic philosophy prior to his conversion emerged as an able apologist for the Christian faith. Chadwick explains, 'Justin was well aware of the existence of Gnostic heresies and wrote a (lost) treatise refuting them.'[317] Irenaeus of Lyons also wrote in opposition to these heresies and Chadwick explains, 'Irenaeus directed his polemic principally against Marcion and Valentinus. His anti-Marcionite argument followed the line laid down by Justin . . . from whose works he gives important quotations.'[318]

From these few brief examples, those who followed on from the first apostles were involved in both a pastoral role and that of defending the faith against heresy. In the post-New Testament writings there is nothing that supports a ministry consisting exclusively of pairs of homeless ministers. It would be difficult to conclude that there is any similarity between the 2x2 ministry and that of the New Testament or first-century church.

[315] Frend, W.H.C, *The Early Church*, 3rd edition, (London: SCM Press, 2003), 251.
[316] Klein, Blomberg and Hubbard, *Biblical Interpretation*, 111.
[317] Chadwick, Henry, *The Early Church*, (London: Penguin Books), 1993, 77.
[318] Chadwick, *Early Church*, 80.

The Church in the Home

The church in the home is a very important tenet of the 2x2 beliefs and references to it are a regular occurrence in their preaching. Because it is such a distinctive feature of the 2x2 movement, it is important to consider this in historical perspective. In the present house churches start for various reasons. Sometimes a schism occurs within a congregation and the breakaway group starts meeting in a home. At times a house church may start as a result of a church plant within a major housing development, this being an interim arrangement until a building is obtained. There are several examples of churches that started in the home and as the numbers increased this necessitated a building with more space.

The house church is by no means a modern phenomenon but goes back to the first century when it was the main assembly point for believers. Until the age of Constantine, church buildings as we know them today did not exist on a large scale. 'Until the end of the third century, the exterior appearance of church buildings was quite undistinguished. Christians gathered in private houses for worship. If they met in larger buildings, these were located in garden areas which hid them from the public.'[319]

The 2x2s will use every reference they can find in Scripture, regardless of how tenuous or out of context, to support the idea of 'only the church in the home'. From the New Testament is evident that initially believers continued to worship in the temple as well as the church in the home. Dunn points out, 'We should not deduce from the few explicit mentions of "the church in someone's house" (Romans 16:5; 1 Corinthians 16:19; Colossians 4:15; Philemon 2) that these refer to house groups, only part of larger congregations.'[320]

The 2x2 argument that no church buildings existed until Constantine is not sustainable given various archaeological discoveries. The discovery

---

[319] Aland, Kurt, *A History of Christianity*, 181.
[320] Dunn, James, 'Is there evidence for fresh expressions of church in the New Testament?' Croft, Steven, editor, *Mission-shaped Questions*, (London: Church House Publishing, 2008), 61.

of the Hellenistic city of Dura Europos destroyed by the Sassanians around 256-57 in an archaeological dig in the twentieth century undermines this argument. Of the discovery, MacCulloch writes: 'the twin revelation of the world's oldest known surviving synagogue and oldest known surviving church building, both survived when buried in earth defences in the final siege, some decades after their original construction.'[321]

The first-century Christians also had buildings for their meetings. According to MacCulloch, 'One of these little border kingdoms of Syria, Osrhoene, had its capital at Edessa (now Urfa in Turkey), which in fact provides the earliest record of a Christian church building, predating the remains at Dura Europos. We know that it was destroyed in a flood in 201.'[322]

These buildings were simple in nature, and this changed after Constantine when places of Christian worship became resplendent edifices with ornate decorations. It is unlikely that all of the believers accepted this trend and there were those who continued to treasure meeting houses that were simple in character. More than likely many of these believers or their ancestors had made the transition from meeting in a private home to a building for worship. According to the *Handbook of Early Christianity*:

> *The first gatherings of religious groups were often in private homes, and they perhaps continued that way for some time. We are accustomed to thinking of the first generations of Christians meeting in houses for their ritual meal. We are less accustomed to thinking of them meeting in a rented space or small private apartment of an insula. There is no direct archaeological evidence of this, but there is indirect evidence: in Ostia in the insula of Diana one of the ground rooms was adapted decoratively and fitted out as a mithraeum, an indication that specified rooms or areas of buildings could be dedicated for religious purposes.[323]*

---

[321] MacCulloch, Diarmaid, *Christianity: The First Three Thousand Years*, (New York: Viking, 2010), 179.

[322] MacCulloch, *Christianity*, 179.

[323] Blaise, Antony J, Turcotte, Paul-Andre and Duhaime, Jean, editors, *Handbook of Early Christianity*, (Oxford: AltaMira Press, 2002), 95.

Nowhere in the New Testament is there any guidance or command as to where the church should meet and according to Tidball meeting places varied according to the need. He writes, 'although public and synagogue proclamation took place, most witnessing was based on private households . . . once a nucleus existed, various strategies existed to form them into a community.'[324]

Many Christians mistakenly refer to the building as the 'church' but such usage is without warrant. Throughout the New Testament, the Greek word *ekklesia* (church) simply means 'assembly'. Scripture presents the church as the people of God, the community and body of Christ, and the fellowship of the Holy Spirit. William Barclay explains what the word *ekklesia* meant to the early disciples:

> *It was the convened assembly of the people . . . the ecclesia directed the policy of the city. It declared war, made peace, contracted treaties and arranged alliances. It elected generals and other military officers. It assigned troops to different campaigns and despatched them from the city. It was ultimately responsible for the conduct of all military operations . . . its two great watchwords were 'equality' and 'freedom'. It was an assembly where everyone had an equal right and an equal duty to take part.*[325]

Even a cursory reading of the New Testament teaches that Jesus and the first-century Christians continued to worship in the synagogue and this did not seem to present any particular difficulty. Dunn supports this and writes, 'so far as we can tell the earliest Christians in Palestine maintained the traditions of Jewish worship virtually unchanged. They attended the temple daily (Acts 2.46; 3.1; 5.12, 21, 42).'[326] A view supported by Stott who writes, 'it is perhaps surprising that they continued for a while in the temple, but they did. They did not immediately abandon the institutional church.'[327] Three other examples from Scripture are, firstly from Jesus, 'Jesus answered him, I spake openly to the world; I ever[328] taught in the synagogue, and in the temple, whither the Jews

---

324   Tidball, *Ministry by the* Book, 100.
325   Barclay, William, *New Testament Words*, (London, SCM, 1964), 68-69.
326   Dunn, *Unity and Diversity*, 127.
327   Stott, *Acts*, 85.
328   Both the ESV and NIV translate this as always.

always resort; and in secret have I said nothing' (John 18:20). Secondly, in Luke 24:53, 'and they were continually in the temple, praising and blessing God. Amen.' Thirdly, in Acts 13:14 Paul and his company are in the synagogue on the Sabbath day. While the 2x2 workers use every possible reference to support the idea of only the church in the home, they ignore and fail to make any attempt to explain how Acts 5:12 should be interpreted. This single verse is important in that it indicates an alternative meeting place of the believers and for clarity, it is important to consider three versions, KJV, ESV and NIV for the latter part of the verse. 'And by the hands of the apostles were many signs and wonders wrought among the people; and they were all of one accord in Solomon's porch' (KJV); 'And they were all together in Solomon's portico' (ESV); 'And the believers used to meet together in Solomon's Colonnade' (NIV).[329]

There is only one interpretation applicable to the second part of this verse and that is that Solomon's porch was a meeting place of the believers. While there is no evidence in the New Testament that the early believers ever constructed a building especially for meeting, there is evidence, as in Acts 5:12 that they did not exclusively meet in homes.

The church in the home has always been a feature of Christianity, in the early church and succeeding periods. The early Baptists met in homes as Underwood writes, 'they often met in the homes of their church-officers and so had no permanent meeting-house.'[330] In the eighteenth century, there was the effectiveness of the house meetings in the development of Methodism. According to Dunn, 'Methodism is a classic example of a renewal movement within Christianity. . . Disowned by the established Church they found a reality and vitality of church in their home-based 'societies'; they discovered the house church.'[331] Methodist services and class meetings met in homes.

Coalter describing the early fellowship meetings of the 2x2s writes, 'they broke bread and testified after a fashion of the love feasts of early

---

[329] A porch along the inner side of the wall enclosing the outer court.
[330] Underwood, A.C, *A History of the English Baptists*, (London: Carey Kingsgate Press, 1947), 127
[331] Dunn, James, Is there evidence of fresh expressions of church in the New Testament. 65

Methodism.'[332] Historically it is fair to say that the house church has been a feature of Christianity since New Testament times. For the 2x2s, the church in the home is for the Sunday morning fellowship and mid-week meeting and is restricted to members only. Certainly, there are no indications from the Book of Acts that the lack of meeting houses curtailed the New Testament church from growing substantially, starting in Jerusalem on the Day of Pentecost and expanding from there. The fact that the New Testament church had no purpose-built places of worship is hardly a reason, on theological grounds, to oppose meeting houses that emerged since the early church and into the twenty-first century.

It would be impossible to conclude from Scripture that there is support only for small numbers of believers meeting in house churches. The 2x2s take the words of Jesus as support, 'For where two or three are gathered in my name, there am I among them' (Matthew 18:26), as a pattern for the meeting of believers in the future but this is taking the words out of context. In contrast, there are those who returned to the upper room following Jesus' ascension and were staying there devoting themselves to prayer and the number was around one hundred and twenty. (Acts 1:12-15). The 2x2s will argue that this was a house church but this seems highly unlikely because of the size of a house and an upper room that would accommodate such a large number. Dunn posits, 'there was sufficient ambiguity in Jesus' teaching about worship for divergent interpretation and practices to emerge almost from the first.'[333]

---

[332] Coalter, *My Memoirs*, 55.
[333] Dunn, James D. G, *Unity and Diversity in the New Testament*, (London: SCM Press, 1977), 127.

The Bible

For the evangelical Christian, Scripture is the rule of faith and practice. Stonehouse emphasises the importance of Scripture when he writes, 'in the fulfilment of the grand and comprehensive plan of redemption the gracious action of the Holy Spirit God has met the need of his people by providing them with the inestimable blessing of the written word.'[334] The constant appeal to Scripture to support belief means the interpretation of what the written word means. On New Testament interpretation Dunn points out that for some interpretation is a purely descriptive exercise and for others it is a prescriptive role. Dunn writes, 'it would be all too easy to develop these two perspectives as polar alternatives, to save ourselves further trouble by simply labelling them respectively "liberal" and "conservative". That done, we could then each retreat safely into our theological and ecclesiastical traditions and either ignore the other or snipe away at the other's exposed flanks.'[335] The 2x2s mainly ignore the prescriptive Scriptures and use the descriptive parts as the *raison d'être* for the movement. Their approach to Scripture is one of pick and mix. They ignore the parts that conflict with their beliefs. If this study were examining another religious movement, it would have the benefit of having access to primary documents. Because the 2x2s have never made any written record as to what they believe this study will use whatever sources that are available. These will range from statements taken from the preaching of workers at missions and conventions to information provided by former members and even some current members and workers. Within this context, we need to examine the place of tradition, inspiration and hermeneutics.

[334] Stonehouse, N. B, 'Special Revelation As Scriptural' in Henry, Carl F.H, editor, *Revelation And The Bible*, (London: Tyndale Press, 1959), 75-76
[335] Dunn, James, D. G, *The Living Word*, (London, SCM Press, 1987), 4-5.

Tradition, Inspiration and Hermeneutics

The Christian tradition has generally subscribed to four sources of theology. These are Scripture, Tradition, Faith and Reason. The Reformed tradition gives Scripture pre-eminence and unless the views posited by tradition, faith and reason can be fully supported by Scripture then they are unacceptable. The Roman Catholic Church differs in that it gives Scripture and Tradition equal importance. The 2x2s claim that what they believe is based solely on the Scriptures. It is reasonable to expect that their beliefs and practices find support in Scripture. Is their use of Scripture and interpretation of Scripture correct? Workers teach that there is total continuity in the movement on a worldwide scale with workers and members working in concert but given the cultural differences alone this seems an unlikely scenario. Stone thinks the problem is that there is no clear understanding of the movement's beliefs and writes, 'I believe the workers, especially the younger workers don't know what the doctrine of the church is, beyond meetings in the home and the two by two ministry.'[336]

For the 2x2s according to Daniel, 'the Bible is a "dead book" unless orally interpreted through one of their "Workers".'[337] Apart from a few favourite texts used as pretexts the movement has scant regard for Scripture as the inspired Word of God. In discussion with 2x2 workers, they avoid engaging with Scripture that may undermine what they teach. For example, to support the 2x2 homeless and unsalaried ministry they will always refer to Matthew 10: 5-15. They are firmly of the opinion that one can only find salvation through one of their preachers and to justify this they will point to John 1:6, 'there was a man sent from God, whose name was John' and Romans 10: 14b-15a, 'and how shall they hear without a preacher? And how shall they preach, except they be sent'? The workers believe that they are the only ones who are sent and that they are the 'true messengers'. Gamble confirmed for me that they believe that they are present day apostles in

....

[336] Stone, *Church Without A Name*, 158.
[337] Daniel, *Reinventing the Truth*, 20.

123

direct succession to the apostles of the New Testament. When asked, what of those from the time of the New Testament church until the arrival of the movement in 1897, he posited that there were more than likely others who carried the work on in that period. When pressed for a more specific answer he replied, 'I don't like to think about it.'[338]

The 2x2s believe that the Bible is the inspired Word of God but they add to this in that they believe that through the Spirit (rarely do they preface this with Holy) only the workers are divinely inspired to interpret Scripture. Bray cautions, 'the inner witness of the Holy Spirit is fundamental to all true Christianity, but it is not exclusive.'[339] One should not underplay the importance in the help of the Holy Spirit to illuminate Scripture but it is important to heed this warning regarding the 2x2 or any similar approach. 'While this approach to biblical interpretation may reflect a commendable confidence in God, it reveals a simplistic (and potentially dangerous) understanding of the illumination of the Holy Spirit and the clarity of Scripture . . . the role of the Spirit in understanding God's Word is indispensable.'[340]

When interpreting Scripture why is hermeneutics important? Hermeneutics is simply the theory of interpretation and 'biblical hermeneutics is a specific area which concerns the interpretation, understanding and appropriation of biblical texts. . . hermeneutics raises prior and more fundamental questions about the very nature of the language, meaning, communication and understanding.'[341] In simple terms, 'hermeneutics provides us with a strategy that will enable us to understand what an author or speaker intended to communicate.'[342]

Scripture will be misinterpreted if the principles of interpretation are flawed or non-existent. Interpretation of Scripture by the 2x2s lacks any principles of interpretation and this is evident from their

---

[338] Discussion with Tommie Gamble 13th February 2012.
[339] Bray, Gerald, *Biblical Interpretation: Past and Present*, (Downers Grove: Inter Varsity Press, 1996). 15
[340] Klein, Blomberg and Hubbard, *Biblical Interpretation*, 4
[341] Thiselton, A. C, 'Hermeneutics' in Ferguson, Sinclair B and Wright David F, editors, *New Dictionary of Theology*, (Leicester: Inter-Varsity Press, 1988), 293.
[342] Klein, Blomberg and Hubbard, *Biblical Interpretation*, 6.

preaching. They rely heavily on the New Testament and on the Gospels in particular. According to Crow:[343]

> It [2x2s] uses the New Testament as its exclusive guide, holding the Old Testament to be a "closed covenant" which God gave to the Jews and which was fulfilled when Christ came. The Old Testament is read and studied for its wisdom and is sometimes discussed in meetings, but it is understood to have been entirely superseded by the New Testament.[344]

Some of the conclusions arrived at by Crow are at variance with the knowledge and experience of others. Crow states, 'the Church is not much removed from the main stream of Protestant theology, although it emphasizes somewhat different things.'[345] This is not an accurate assessment of its theological position. In reaching this conclusion Crow draws heavily on his own personal background with the 2x2s although he was not a member of the movement. His grandparents and his mother were 2x2s in the State of Oregon and his research reflects what went on there. Because of this limitation, we may find that his conclusions may not generally be true of the wider world of 2x2s. Crow writes:

> By comparison with other primitive Christian sects, The Church [2x2s] appears to be highly sophisticated and intellectual in its reading and interpretation of the Scriptures, while at the same time it remains at an extreme of asceticism. The workers are excellent Bible scholars, devoting much time to study and exegesis of the New Testament. They clearly understand that the gospels have been through many vicissitudes of translation, and they avoid hairsplitting analysis of the precise meaning of particular words and phrases. Their concern is for general "spiritual" rather than literal meaning.[346]

---

[343] Crow's thesis is written mainly from a sociological perspective and engages only minimally with theological aspects of the movement.
[344] Crow, *Invisible Church*. Thesis. Pages unnumbered.
[345] Crow, *Invisible Church*, Thesis. Pages unnumbered.
[346] Crow, *Invisible Church*, Thesis. Pages unnumbered.

Over the past three years of this research, I have attended many meetings and listened to many sermons and I have yet to hear a sermon that was either topical or exegetical. The preaching is generally vague and without application.

There is little, if any, evidence of scholarship in the preaching of the workers. Writing on the preaching of 2x2 workers Stone says, 'rather than make direct statements regarding their doctrine, they talk around the subject, quoting clichés and scripture, telling several stories and ending up with an implication.'[347]

When Crow describes the workers as Bible scholars it would have been useful if he could have let us have examples of some scholarly output since the absence of evidence makes this difficult to accept. I have known labourers and others who never had any formal education who can stand shoulder to shoulder with men of great academic achievement when it comes to expounding the Scriptures. It is difficult for a man or woman to fit the description of a Bible scholar capable of sound exegesis if they are without a knowledge of the Bible languages of Hebrew and Greek, or never studied church history and are not permitted to read any book except the Bible.

The lack of hermeneutics is clear in examples of sermons that I have heard preached at various missions and conventions. One example of this is on page 98 where a worker at the Fermanagh convention manages to interpret the fish gate in Nehemiah 3:3 as a basis for the 2x2 ministry. A Canadian worker, Jason Pearman speaking at the Stockholm convention read from Matthew 7: 24-27, the account of the wise man building his house on the rock and the foolish man building his house on the sand. His opening words were:

> *I would like to speak a little bit about sanctuaries and a sanctuary is a place of refuge or of safety. There is a city in Canada, it's a big city and it is very busy. But right in the middle of that city there is a bird sanctuary and that is a safe place for those birds to live. And there are sanctuaries that we can have that are safe places for us. I never really thought of Jesus words being like sanctuary. But this says when the storm comes they will keep us.*[348]

---

[347] Stone, *Church Without A Name*, 213.
[348] Jason Pearman, Stockholm convention, Friday morning, 22nd July 2011.

He continued and preached how the birds find sanctuary in the mustard tree; Mary and Joseph provided a sanctuary for Jesus in their home and how the beaver in Canada finds sanctuary in the dam that it builds. He ended his sermon:

> *And your homes are also sanctuaries for us workers. Abraham had a tent but the servants of God found rest in his home. Lot had a house but the servants of God never had rest in his home. So it is not the natural comforts that make your home a sanctuary. It is a sanctuary when we can find rest for our soul in your home. And I would like to mention about the meeting [Sunday morning fellowship meeting] it is a sanctuary too. It is how God has planned things. So it is our motives when we go to meetings is to feel and to make it a safe place And when we are humbled by the presence of the emblems it is a safe place Sometimes we might think of something that someone else needs to hear but if we just bring that, that is like bringing a stone but when we apply a message to ourselves that is like bringing grace. It doesn't take any effort to find a stone but it does take an effort to bring grace. So being accepted is such a part of making life a place a sanctuary. And I hope we will use these sanctuaries that God has provided.*[349]

From beginning to end, this sermon consisted of many disconnected ideas and it is difficult to understand the connection between the passage and the message. Preaching at a mission in Portadown, Herbie Jennings read Matthew 16: 13-20, the account of Peter's confession of Christ. From the words, 'that thou art Peter, and upon this rock I will build my church; and the gates of hell shall not prevail against it', Jennings managed to interpret this as a condemnation of church buildings and support for the church in the home:

> *He [Jesus] said in vain they do worship me, teaching for doctrines the commandments of men. So they were taking the commandments of men and they were making a doctrine out of it. And said, that's the teaching now, lets (sic) go with that. And they readjusted the thing the way they want. They turn the thing around. I don't want to be, I don't want to be sarcastic when I say this but that's how buildings*

---

[349] Pearman, Stockholm convention, Friday morning, 22nd July 2011.

came on the scene, and that's why the church was called a building. It was because man got the idea that he'd build a church and it would be a lot handier, it would be a lot more convenient because we won't have to open our homes and we won't have people coming and gathering in our homes anymore. We'll just get this building and set it up and we'll say that's the house of God and we'll be organised. But wouldn't it be an awful thing, wouldn't it an awful thing (sic) if we spent the rest of our days worshipping God and it's all in vain. It would be an awful thing, really, worshipping God and the whole thing is in vain. It's of no advantage, no advantage to ourselves, God's grieved, because it's not His, according to His plan, it's not according to His plan, it would grieve Him. And how could God be into that, how could God be in that. But we're glad, we're glad, God's perfect truth and God's perfect plan that the gates of hell will not prevail against it, the gates of hell won't power over it.[350]

Jennings then moved on through his sermon and finished off using examples of the church in the home in the New Testament:

Do you know something else interesting about the church is that, I took a little note of it, and the, in Corinthians, (sic) [Romans 16] it says Greet Pricilla and Aquila in the church in your, in their house, Narcissus and the church in his house, what was the other one, Narcissus and the church in his house, and then there's a another one, Aristobulus, that's how you pronounce it, in the church in his house. That is interesting to me, and its emphasis that Paul, Saul as Jack was speaking about, that in his day before he got saved, before he got the truth within him, before he had the revelation of the truth, he was persecuting the church. He was going from house to house, and hauling men and women out and committing them to prison. So house to the house where the church was and he was going into the church, into those homes, into those houses, and taking out those and committing them to prison.[351]

These examples are not selections of the worst but are truly representative of the 2x2 workers' handling of Scripture. In discussion

---

350 Herbie Jennings, mission in Corcrain Community Centre, Portadown, 21st March 2011.
351 Herbie Jennings, mission in Corcrain Community Centre, Portadown, 21st March 2010.

with a former 2x2 I asked how intelligent people can listen to such poor preaching. He replied, 'remember they are at meetings because they must be there and they switch off and don't even hear what is being preached.'[352] Teaching is obviously poor and this must lead to the lack of solid knowledge of biblical theology by the members.

When the 2x2s say they believe the Bible their Bible knowledge is so superficial that they are incapable of communicating the basic tenets of Christianity McDermott points out, 'the best of evangelical theology believes that the language of Scripture is culturally conditioned but that through it God has nevertheless conveyed the eternal, unconditional Word.'[353] The authority of Scripture has a historical basis that was in place long before the term evangelical was currency. According to Henry, 'the church fathers nowhere attribute error to inspired Scripture, whether Old Testament or New; the truthfulness of the sacred writings is regarded in the divine authority and inspiration.'[354] According to Parker, 'they seem to have adopted, in exaggerated form, the old opinion of an inner illumination and regard the Bible apart from their interpretation of their experience as simply a dead book.'[355] It has the appearance of the Gnosticism that was prevalent in the early church era. The absence of soundly based principles of interpretation of Scripture will obviously influence the way 2x2s view other major doctrines of the Christian faith.

Whatever they really believe as to the inspiration of Scripture they do not believe that Scripture alone is sufficient to lead to salvation. They ignore 'and that from a child thou has known the holy scriptures, which are able to make thee wise unto salvation through faith which is in Christ Jesus' (2 Timothy 3:15). The Scriptures make one wise to salvation, not the medium of the 2x2 worker.

---

[352] Discussion in Belfast, 18th February 2012.
[353] McDermott, *Can Evangelicals learn?* 30.
[354] Kantzer, Kenneth S. and Henry, Carl E. H, editors, *Evangelical Affirmations*, (Grand Rapids: Zondervan, 1990), 82
[355] Parker, *Secret Sect*, 105.

The Church

What the wider Christian world refers to as the doctrine of ecclesiology has no part in the 2x2 thinking. Fortt states the church is, 'the local body of people who gather in a home (meeting) to "break bread;" only those of "The Truth." Thus, each individual group, meeting in a home, is referred to as a church.' [356] Fortt is referring to the Sunday morning fellowship meeting and this is a closed meeting for members only. Stone writes, 'the workers ask professing people NOT to bring unprofessing people to fellowship meetings. . . the friends may reveal doctrine and attitudes that the workers want hidden.'[357] Quite simply the doctrine of the church is the homeless ministry and the church in the home. For the 2x2 as long as these two features are present then everything else is in order.

The movement gives no recognition to the various offices in the Church such as those that Paul outlines to the Ephesians: 'And he gave some, apostles; and some, prophets; and some evangelists; and some, pastors and teachers; For the perfecting of the saints, for the work of the ministry, for the edifying the body of Christ' (Ephesians 4: 11-12). It is not facetious to note the absence of 'workers' in Paul's list of offices, but without any authority from Scripture, they will contend that their workers fulfil these roles.

The Trinity

One of the most important doctrines of the Christian faith is the doctrine of the Trinity - there is one true God revealed as three persons; God the Father, God the Son and God the Holy Spirit. The Trinitarian doctrine is not overtly stated in the Bible and 'Trinity' is a secondary word with a long history dating back to the late second century, first used by Tertullian.[358] 'Christians of all ages and branches affirm

---

[356]   Fortt, *Search for "the Truth"*, 41.
[357]   Stone, *Church Without A Name*, 160.
[358]   Hall, Stuart G, *Doctrine and Practice in the Early Church*, (London: SPCK, 1991), 72.

that there is no God but the Lord, who is Father, Son and Spirit.'[359]
McGrath supports this view when he writes:

> *Evangelicalism is historic Christianity. Its beliefs correspond to the*
> *central doctrines of the Christian churches down through the ages,*
> *including the two most important doctrine of the patristic period: the*
> *doctrine of the 'two natures', human and divine, of Jesus Christ and*
> *the doctrine of the Trinity.[360]*

It is therefore, essential that the doctrine of the Trinity has a prominent
place in the statement of beliefs of any church that claims to be
evangelical. The doctrine of the Trinity remains difficult for some
to grasp and this is not peculiar to those of the twenty-first century
as Augustine explains, 'when we think about God, the trinity we are
aware that our thoughts are quite inadequate to their object, and quite
incapable of grasping him as he is.'[361]

According to Long's diary for March 1898, William Irvine embraced
the doctrine of the Trinity: 'Concerning the principles of the Doctrine
of Christ, he was sound. He believed in the fall of man, in the
Atonement, in the Trinity, in the Divinity of our Lord.'[362] The doctrine
of the Trinity is rejected by most in the 2x2 movement although in
fairness there are those who believe it. It is in situations such as this that
the absence of any statement of faith leads to confusion. There are on
record statements such as that made by worker, Doug Morse, speaking
on 'The Holy Spirit' at 2nd Pilerwa convention, Australia, 2011:

> *Everything we've learned and enjoyed has been revealed to us through*
> *the Spirit during this "engagement period" of our marriage to the*
> *Bridegroom. What better one to do this but the Spirit? We read of*
> *the Father, the Son, and the Holy Ghost, three separate Beings. In*
> *the world there is a belief that this is one Being and it is spoken of*
> *as the Trinity. This is a manmade term and is wrong doctrine. A*
> *man named Constantine, in 300 AD introduced this idea to try*

359 Driscoll and Breshears, *Vintage Church*, 191.
360 McGrath, *Evangelicalism and the Future*, 94.
361 Quoted in Johnson, Keith E, 'Augustine', *Trinity Journal*, Volume 32 NS, No. 2, Fall 2011, 163.
362 Long's diary.

to bring some unity in these already splintering groups. Col 2:9 speaks of the Godhead. (Also Acts 17:29, Romans 1:20) "For in Him dwelleth all the fullness of the Godhead bodily." God did not die on the Cross, and the Spirit did not rise from the sepulcher; it was Jesus. To understand it a little better, it is like the clock on that post. It has three separate hands working together, in perfect unity. The Father, the Son, and the Holy Ghost have an Oneness that we can't comprehend with the human mind. But they are three separate Beings. We can't subtract one from the other. They all serve separately but maybe one day will blended so perfectly.[363]

Parker writes:

From sources available it appears that Christ is seen as having been neither the perfect man nor the perfect God, but as a pattern preacher, and it has been evident in discussion with sectarians that they do not hold the doctrine of the divinity of Christ as is believed by Christian denominations who teach His pre-existence as God's eternal Word through whom all things were created.[364]

The Deity of Christ and the doctrine of the Trinity are inextricably linked and a flawed view of one negates the other. Many senior workers are on record as denigrating the doctrine of the Trinity and Fortt provides a few examples. Speaking at a meeting in Los Angeles on 10th March 1985 a senior worker, Dan Hilton, said, 'the word Trinity is not found in the Bible. It is a Catholic doctrine that wasn't mentioned by the early Christians.[365] It wasn't heard of until the second century'. While another worker, Dale Bors[366] in Sacramento, California in 1979 stated, 'it depends who we are talking to whether we believe in the Trinity or not'. That ambiguity certainly erodes trust in the workers' words. Stone recalls hearing, 'brother workers in gospel meetings speak against the idea of Jesus being fully God and fully man. They said he was half God and half man. Others have insisted that he is fully man filled with the SPIRIT.'[367]

---

[363] http://www.trutharchive.net/doug-morse---the-holy-spirit---2nd-pilerwa-australia---2011. Accessed 10th February 2012.
[364] Parker, *Secret Sect*, 101.
[365] Early Christians for the 2x2 movement means New Testament Christians.
[366] Fortt, *Search For "The Truth"*, 182-183.
[367] Stone, *Church Without A Name*, 170.

One correspondent who professed at age sixteen testified, 'I felt assured that all the sins I repented of would be forgiven and that if I let the Spirit guide me, I would live in accordance with the teachings of Jesus.'[368] On the doctrine of the Trinity, this person posted:

> *As far as I am concerned, people are free to have their own conviction as to the Trinity . . . The workers don't preach the Trinity: that's been made abundantly clear here. . . Some days I believe in the Trinity and some days I don't. Last I checked, God still loved me and was working in my life. Our Lord said being born again was the key to entering the kingdom, not whether or not we could answer the Trinity question correctly at the Pearly Gates.*[369]

This statement views the doctrine of the Trinity as unimportant. Many other 2x2s take a similar view and this may be because they lack knowledge and fail to understand the importance of clarity on the doctrine of the Trinity. Thompson stresses its importance when he writes, 'Christian theology cannot conceive of God apart from Jesus Christ so it can neither dispense with the doctrine of the Trinity or treat is as an appendix with no real connection to its other interests.'[370] Bailey relates an interesting discussion that took place over dinner with a colleague and an Egyptian Muslim Scholar. She asked. 'Gentlemen, can one of you explain the Christian doctrine of the Trinity to me? I have been trying to find an explanation that I can understand for twenty-five years and I have failed. Can you help me'? Bailey describes how he responded:

> *I offered a brief discussion on the text before us [1 Corinthians 2: 10b-11, 15-16] with its Pauline parable of the human person. I told my questioner that in the Qur'an one can read about "God," "the Word of God," and the "Spirit of God." The Islamic tradition has chosen not to reflect on how those three come together. That choice is their privilege, and I respect their freedom in that decision, I told her. But in the Christian tradition we also have God, his Word and his Spirit, and we have chosen to reflect how these thee form a unity.*

---

[368]   Private message 10th July 2010.
[369]   http://professing.proboards.com/index.cgi?board=general&action=display&thread=1884 5&page=1. Posted and accessed, 10th February 2012.
[370]   Thompson, Mark D, *A Clear and Present Word*, (Nottingham: Apollos, 2006), 50-51.

> *Greatly relieved the professor replied, "At last! Someone has given me an explanation of the Trinity I can understand. I am so grateful." I quickly assured her that thanks were not due to me, but due to St. Paul, who gave us the text (with its parable).*[371]

With the 2x2 emphasis on the homeless ministry and the church in the home, major doctrines of the Christian faith are often avoided. There is a reluctance to approach Scripture with an open mind and instead they tend to stick with a few texts that they believe support what they want to believe. Bailey's account gives a clear and simple explanation of the Trinitarian doctrine and he concludes, 'the mystery of the Trinity and the cross are folly to the natural man. The believer is responsible to *receive, understand* and finally *impart* the *mysteries* of God to others.'[372] By rejecting or not teaching the doctrine of the Trinity workers are neglecting to address a major tenet of the Christian faith. There is sufficient evidence that this is the situation within the 2x2 movement; although some do believe the doctrine this is not enough to influence the movement overall. This is a doctrine of first importance and not a secondary doctrine where there is some room for personal interpretation. The importance of the doctrine of the Trinity from the early church and throughout history is summarised by Jeyachandran who writes:

> *An overwhelming number of Scriptures attribute full divinity to all three persons. Thus the early church is driven to the only option: that these three distinct persons in some way constitute the one divine being. Over the next centuries the church came to articulate the doctrine of God as Trinity − a word not found in canonical Scriptures − by semantically combining both the unity of the essence of the Godhead and the three distinct personalities of Father, Son, and Holy Spirit.*[373]

---

[371] Bailey, Kenneth, *Paul, Through Mediterranean Eyes*, (London: SPCK, 2011), 115.
[372] Bailey, *Paul*, 119.
[373] Jeyachandran, L. T, 'The Trinity as a Paradigm for Spiritual Transformation' in Zacharias, Ravi, editor, *Beyond Opinion*, (Nashville: Thomas Nelson, 2007), 236-237.

The Cross

The nature of the atonement is a topic debated by Christian scholars but it is important to let Scripture be the arbiter on this important subject. There are so many Scriptures to support the efficacy of the Christ's death on the cross for the sin of humanity and we will just use one, 'for our sake he made him to be sin who knew no sin, so that in in him we might become the righteousness of God' (2 Corinthians 5:21). This reference would arguably point to penal substitution. Commenting on this verse, Jeffrey, Ovey and Sach state:

> *This emphasis on the imputation of our guilt to Christ and his righteousness to us amounts to a statement of penal substitution. If we sideline it, we risk distorting the biblical picture of reconciliation.*[374]

For evangelicals in the past and present, the cross is central to what they believe and evangelicalism embodies this centrality. McGrath points out:

> *Evangelicalism places an especial emphasis on the centrality of the cross of Christ. The cross is the unique and perfect sacrifice which covers and shields us from the righteous anger of God against sin, reconciles us to God and opens the way to the glorious freedom of the children of God.*[375]

One rarely hears a reference to the cross or the blood of the Lord Jesus Christ in 2x2 preaching. I have asked specifically as to what workers believe regarding the blood of Christ and why they cannot give clarity in gospel meetings. When referring to the gospel why not say that it is a call to repentance, through faith in Christ and cleansing in the blood of the Lamb. Why is there not a clear definition in every meeting as to what the gospel is?

> *The senior worker said that they spend hours before a meeting preparing for the meeting, they never write anything down. They prepare their hearts and ask God for the message and they never*

---

[374] Jeffrey, Steve, Ovey, Mike and Sach, Andrew, *Pierced for our Transgressions*, (Nottingham: IVP, 2007), 143.
[375] McGrath, *Evangelicalism and the Future*, 62.

*prepare a text for any meeting. This is the same for all meetings –
conventions, special meetings, fellowship meetings, gospel meetings or
funerals. Workers are entirely dependent upon what God gives them
when they stand up there. At the end of the meeting 'we bow our head
and thank God that he gave us a message from heaven. . . . In one
night in the gospel meeting that is why you cannot get the full story.
The card says 'the story of Jesus' but we can only cover a tiny part
in one meeting. He referred to one night in Dromore when that night
it was sin, repentance and the blood. He concluded, 'It is a story that
unfolds page by page, chapter by chapter.'* [376]

This answer lacked substance and I needed further clarification and
requested a further meeting so that I could address the topic in more
depth. I was somewhat taken aback by the reply I got, 'Regarding
your suggestion to meet again for further discussion, presently I as yet
haven't felt the draw of God's Spirit that this is necessary, as we told
you we wait on direction from God. If at any later time we feel moved,
we will contact you.'[377] With all due respect to the leading of 'God's
Spirit' I do not accept that in such circumstances one can know for
certainty the leading and guidance of the Holy Spirit. This at best was
a plausible excuse for not wanting to face up to further questions.

Since they reject the divinity of Christ, Parker posits, 'it follows that
a comparatively limited view of Christ is held in the areas of the
doctrines of the incarnation and the purpose of the atonement.'[378]
Parker has studied the movement extensively, and is well qualified to
make this pronouncement. Commenting on the movement's view on
the blood of Christ, Stone writes:

*The early workers regularly mocked the belief in the sufficiency of
the blood of Christ to wash away man's sin. They said "it is the
life that is necessary, not the blood". They said that, "if it was just
the blood that redeemed men then Jesus would have been put to death
at birth". They preached that one had to give his life as Jesus did
in the ministry or else follow the ministry that did as he did. . . It*

[376] Meeting with two workers 20th January 2012
[377] Email 31st January 2012.
[378] Parker, *Secret Sect*, 102.

isn't that they don't believe in the blood of Christ. They just don't (sic) believe in its sufficiency. That means that they don't believe that Christ's blood is able to cleanse the sins of mankind unless people do something to earn it.[379]

One of the most explicit statements is from a senior worker in the US, Leo Stancliff, who said, 'my hope of salvation is the blood of Christ. But I would like to explain to you what it means. The blood of Christ is the ministry and the church in the home. Without the New Testament ministry you don't have the blood of Christ which includes the church in the home. The forgiveness of sins is a fringe benefit.'[380] This teaching is so far out of line with biblical doctrines of the atonement that it is difficult to understand how following such a statement he is permitted to remain in the work, that is unless he was vocalising their true position. It is disconcerting that this view is expressed by a senior worker and not by one who is young and inexperienced.

The efficacy of the blood of Christ in the plan of salvation is obviously denied at least by some in the movement and others are at best ambiguous as to what they believe on penal substitution. This is supported by Stone who writes, 'they simply disguise it [their views] by saying that there are conditions one must meet in order to have the cleansing of the blood.'[381] It would be best to summarise their view as the blood plus and the plus is the 2x2 ministry and the church in the home.

[379] Stone, *Church Without A Name*, 124.
[380] http://www.workersect.org/2x205g.html. Accessed 18th February 2012.
[381] Stone, *Church Without A Name*, 125.

The Gospel

The litmus test for any movement is how they define the gospel of Jesus Christ. If their view of the gospel is incoherent, this will lead to all kinds of difficulties. Getting a definition of the gospel from the 2x2s is fraught with difficulty. I agree with Daniel when he writes, 'the "Workers" themselves tend to speak only in vague platitudes and analogies. Most of what is said is couched in orthodox-sounding terminology.'[382] Nevertheless, this orthodox-sounding terminology does not extend to recognising any of the creeds of the early church. For example, those who lay claim to orthodoxy can usually affirm the tenets of the Christian faith as set out in the Apostles Creed:

> *I believe in God, the Father Almighty maker of heaven and earth and in Jesus Christ his only Son our Lord who was conceived by the Holy Ghost born of the Virgin Mary. Suffered under Pontius Pilate, was crucified, dead and buried. He descended into hell. On the third day he rose again from the dead. He ascended into the heaven and sitteth on the right hand of God the Father Almighty. From thence he will come to judge the quick and the dead. I believe in the Holy Ghost, the holy catholic church, the communion of saints, the forgiveness of sins, the resurrection of the body and life everlasting. Amen.*[383]

For Packer the creed is the gospel and he writes, 'I want to display the Creed as, in effect, a power-point declaration of the Christian message – in other words, of the gospel itself.'[384] The 2x2 response to this is, the creed is extra-biblical and therefore they could not accept the veracity of this statement of faith. The Creed is unashamedly Trinitarian and that will create a barrier for many in the 2x2 movement as will its affirmation of the divinity of Christ, another doctrine the movement rejects. Parker points out, 'it has been evident in discussion with sectarians that they do not hold the doctrine of the divinity of Christ.'[385] Jacobsen, a former worker writes, 'I remember very well the day around

---

[382] Daniel, *Reinventing the Truth*, 19.
[383] Bray, *Creeds, Councils and Christ*, 101.
[384] Packer, J. I, *Affirming the Apostles' Creed*, (Wheaton: Crossway, 2008), 15.
[385] Parker, *The Secret Sect*, 101.

our dinner table when I taught them of our Lord's Deity. . . when I told an elder in Sweden they were preaching in various parts of the USA that Christ was not God made flesh, he said shocked, "*NEJ, SAGER DU DET?*" (Do not say that!).'[386] The rejection of this important doctrine makes it increasingly difficult for the 2x2 definition of the gospel to meet the evangelical credentials as defined by Bebbington and the evangelical grouping at large. Packer informs us:

> *What makes an evangelical will be that which in the eyes of the New Testament writers makes a Christian. What is that? In a phrase, it is true faith in the real Jesus Christ. One who does not display this is will only not be an evangelical; the question arises whether they are a Christian at all, and evangelicals will judge that they cannot be unless they are better and sounder at heart than appearances suggest . . . we need to realize that, as the doctrine of the Trinity is not an idle fancy or speculation about God in the abstract but a specific claim about our Lord Jesus Christ, so the doctrine of the Incarnation is not an idle fancy or speculation about Jesus in isolation but a specific claim about God.*[387]

This statement encapsulates what Scripture teaches and evangelicals believe is the heart of Gospel of Jesus Christ the Son of God. Without any agreed statement of faith it becomes apparent that there is little consensus within the movement as to what they really believe. It is difficult to get direct answers as Daniel points out:

> *Two-by-Two ministers do not give direct answers to questions regarding doctrine. They try very hard to be seen as orthodox, particularly by outsiders. Newcomers who ask serious doctrinal questions are usually either told to "just keep coming to the meeting and you will understand," or they are given carefully crafted answers designed not to expose the sect's true beliefs. Apparently, the ministry considers evasion and deception to be acceptable means of winning and keeping converts.*[388]

This vagueness is best illustrated in the preaching at a 2x2 mission

---

[386] Private message from Dennis Jacobsen, 21st December 2011.
[387] Packer, J. I, *Celebrating the Saving Work of God*, (Carlisle: Paternoster, 1998), 75-76.
[388] Daniel, *Reinventing the Truth*, 79.

where the worker, Edgar Lowe, made several references to the Gospel without defining the term. Lowe stated:

I love the simplicity[389] of the way of God. Everything about it is simplicity and truth. There is nothing complicated. Even the youngest child can understand it when the gospel is spoken and people sit and listen under the influence of the spirit of God. We can't convince people. We are not here to convince anyone. No that would be of man. We are here to tell you the truth. We are here to tell you the gospel of Jesus Christ and in telling you the gospel of Jesus Christ, he said not by letter only but by the spirit there is where the thing comes and there is where the secret is, it is the work of the spirit of God that as people listen to the Gospel that is spoken and the spirit of God opens their heart to receive the message they are listening to and open their eyes to understand, this is what I am reading about in the Bible.[390]

The terminology, 'that as people listen to the Gospel that is spoken' is a misnomer because apart from referring to the Gospel, they never say what the Gospel is. Two days later in a discussion with a senior 2x2 who holds the rank of bishop/elder who was at the mission, I asked, 'what is meant by "the Gospel"?' The response was, 'keep coming to the mission and you will get a revelation.'[391] This response sounds similar to Daniel's 'just keep coming to the meeting and you will understand.' I spoke with Lowe about his sermon and use of the term gospel and he responded, 'we are not there to explain how this thing works. We bring a message from God and people get a revelation.'[392]

One former 2x2 woman living in South Africa wrote, 'note that among the Meeting folk, "gospel" has a slightly different meaning to the generally accepted telling of the story of Jesus. It is more of a member-

---

[389] Lowe's preaching stands in contrast to that of J. C. Ryle 'all the simplicity in the world can do no good, unless you preach the simple gospel of Jesus Christ so fully and so clearly that everybody can understand it. If Christ crucified has not his rightful place in your sermons, and sin is not exposed as it should be, and your people are not plainly told what they ought to believe, and be and do, your preaching is no use.' Cited by J. I. Packer in *Faithfulness and Holiness*, (Wheaton: Crossway, 2002), 63.
[390] Richhill mission 22nd November 2011.
[391] Discussion 24th November 2011.
[392] Meeting on 20th January 2012.

recruitment campaign: those who listen are expected to understand that the Workers are the ONLY true servants of God, and that coming into this fellowship is the ONLY true way to heaven.'[393]

The sermons we read in the Acts of the Apostles from Peter and Paul should be a model for apostolic preaching. Each of these sermons presents the gospel with clarity and with conviction. Given that we can read most of these sermons in around two minutes, we must conclude that what Luke has given us is a précis of the original. Even with the précis, we get clarity as to the message. Sermons by 2x2 workers are entirely different from those sermons we find in the New Testament because that is not how the workers preach. After listening to around 50 or more sermons, I agree with Stone who writes, 'one visiting minister to a "Two by Two" meeting said afterwards that he had never heard such a jumble of disconnected ideas in his life.'[394] One simply will never hear a sermon from a worker that remotely resembles those of Peter in Acts 2:14-40 or Paul in Acts 17: 22-31. These sermons are quite different since the audiences were different: Peter for his Jewish listeners and Paul for Stoic and Epicurean philosophers - but both had a message that called for a decision.

The workers' inability to adapt to meet the needs of the listeners means that in this world where postmodernism is to the fore they have nothing to say that makes Scripture relevant and challenging. They fail to recognise that this is a largely an unchurched society and to invite someone from such a background into what the 2x2s say is a gospel meeting would be confusing. With their exclusivism and King James Version English in their prayers and preaching, they would be something of an obstacle.

To the question, 'how 2x2s define the Gospel' there were various responses but the following from a former worker illustrates the 2x2 position and their convoluted thinking:

> *I believe the majority of workers would define "the gospel" as something like this, 'The gospel is the good news of Jesus Christ who lived to show us how to live and died to save and ransom us'.*

[393]   Email 12th October 2008.
[394]   Stone, *Church Without A Name*, 220.

That is what the workers would tell an outsider if they were asked. Those words are probably in line with what the outsider believes, as well. How they define those words is what sets the workers apart. "Jesus lived to show us how to live" means that the "Good News" of the gospel is that Jesus is the same yesterday today and forever .....Meaning that the workers are living the life of Jesus and other preachers clearly aren't.....Meaning that, while the message in other churches might have truths in it, the LIFE that Jesus lived isn't there. So the gospel according to the workers is that not only did Jesus die and all that. He also sent forth disciples into the world to preach the good news in the same Spirit as Jesus. So the workers claim to be preaching in Spirit (having the Holy Spirit) and in Truth (having the true method of ministry according to the truth of the words and teachings of Jesus). You will have to sit through quite a few gospel meetings to get all that out of them, but that is what is meant by their initial statement of faith.[395]

This is what the 2x2s mean by the Gospel and it bears no resemblance to the Gospel recorded in the New Testament. The gospel for the 2x2s is the ministry, homeless workers going out in pairs and the church that meet in the home. According to their line of thought, unless both of these distinctives are present then it is not the gospel.

---

[395] http://professing.proboards.com/index.cgi?board=general&action=display&thread=1880 2&page=2. Accessed 8th February 2012..

Conversion

Christians use the term conversion to describe their coming to faith in Christ. Other terms include 'saved' and 'born again' and all three of these words are found in Scripture. However, in the 2x2 vocabulary, the term is 'professing' and it is important to establish if this equates to the evangelical experience of conversion. To help get an understanding of what professing actually means in practice I asked a few ex-2x2s for their views. One ex-member who professed at fourteen years old said, 'I just stood up at the end of a mission and indicated that I wanted to follow Jesus and join the meetings'. When asked if this involved repentance, she replied, 'no one said anything about that.'[396] A long established member who is a fourth generation 2x2, when asked what professing meant, responded:

> *The idea with the 2 by 2 worker system is that people would listen to the gospel, and at the end of the mission period they would have a chance to respond. If this is positive response then they can take part in a Sunday morning meeting. The next progressive step would be baptism, Acts 18 v 8. Believe first and baptized later. As you know we do not baptize people that are automatically born into the faith. There needs to be an individual submission first.*[397]

An ex-worker from Alabama, US who spent twelve years as a worker made one of the clearest statements on professing. When asked if they had called sinners to repentance, he stated, 'we never in the work did anything like walk people down the Romans road and take them through the steps of salvation. There was never a prayer where they confessed they were a sinner or renounced sin verbally. I am only in the past few years [a reference to his leaving the work] learning about things like that.'[398] Here we have a clear example of one who spent a number of years as a worker and was unfamiliar with the basics of conversion. Following the act of professing the person is required to attend all 2x2 meetings.

....

[396]   Discussion on 19th January 2011.
[397]   Email 27th November 2011.
[398]   Private message 16th January 2011.

143

From the moment a person professes there is pressure on them to participate in the Sunday morning fellowship meetings and failure or reluctance to do so is seen as being unwilling. Many with whom I have spoken have made a profession but there has been no inward change and they found that all they were doing was following the rules and had little or no joy in their life. This is not peculiar to the 2x2 church since there are many in evangelical churches who make a profession without ever coming to faith in Christ, and although they go through the motions of being a Christian, they too have no real joy or peace.

The emphasis in gospel meetings is on following Jesus who is our example instead of preaching of Jesus as Saviour. The reference to following Jesus as the example permeates most prayers and sermons and is either explicit or implicit. The opening prayer[399] at a recent mission illustrates this point:

> *Our Father we give you thanks again this evening for the Bible. This word that we can learn so much from. We are thankful for the example of Jesus and what it means to be following that example. We thank you for those that are moved to leave these things on record for us. We thank you that you are still working in the hearts and lives of people today and people today can still be moved by thy spirit to fulfil thy will in whatever way necessary and to meet whatever needs arise. We thank thee Father for the ministry [2x2 workers] that we can see, first of all in the life of Jesus and those who followed him. We are thankful for this same ministry that we can see today following the same example and we pray Father that thou wouldst continue to help us to follow this example. We know we need thy help and thy power to do this and we pray that thou wouldst again show us and open our eyes to see again you're that example and we would follow faithfully as faithful and humble servants. Father we thank thee that we have this privilege of being able to pray, pray to thee knowing that thou dost listen. And we are thankful Father for the times we have known and been sure that thou hast heard our prayer and hast answered our prayer. Accept our thanks in these things we ask in Jesus name.[400]*

---

399   In their prayers and sermons the workers use KJV terminology as is evident in this prayer.
400   Gospel meeting in Bleary, County Armagh, 9th February 2012.

By rejecting the Deity of Christ, the movement reduces Christ to a good man whose example one can follow. Fully accepting the Deity of Christ and His place in the Trinity means that Christ is Saviour and Redeemer instead of simply being our example. Horton points out:

> *There is a world of difference between having a role model whose example we fall short of ever reproducing and having yourself "killed" and re-created as branches of the Tree of Life. Doing what Jesus did is different from bearing the fruit of Christ's righteous life. In fact, the most important thing that Jesus ever did cannot be duplicated. Because he fulfilled the law in our place, bore our curse and was raised in glory to take his Throne at the Father's right hand, we can have a relationship with him – and with the Father – that is far more intimate than the relationship of a devotee to a guru, a student to a teacher or a follower to a master.*[401]

There is a noticeable absence of preaching that elevates Christ and His work on the cross as sufficient for salvation. Professing for a 2x2 will always mean accepting the ministry and this excerpt from a sermon by a senior worker emphasises this:

> *This matter of a relationship with God, it's not a matter of joining a certain religion; it's not a matter of attaching ourselves to any denomination or sect. It is a matter of a real relationship with God, this is what eternal life is and this is what salvation is, when Jesus comes to remain, by His Spirit. When He comes to dwell in our hearts, when we open our hearts to accept Him and accept His teaching and accept His doctrine and accept His ministry [the workers] and everything that He upholds. When we open our heart to God we're opening our heart to the saviour Jesus.*[402]

In reality, this means accepting Christ plus 2x2 teaching, doctrine and ministry. This is not a Gospel of salvation by grace through faith in Christ alone. Conversion or professing for a 2x2 always means accepting Christ plus their additions.

....

[401] Horton, Michael, *The Gospel-Driven Life*, (Grand Rapids: Baker Books, 2009), 151.
[402] Edgar Lowe, Masonic Hall, Tandragee, March 2011.

Activism and Social Action

This characteristic of evangelicalism is evidenced in many different ways depending upon the emphasis within a church or fellowship. McGrath points out, 'at its heart, evangelicalism has a deep-seated awareness of the importance of Christian community for the tasks of evangelism, spiritual nourishment, teaching and discipling.'[403] Jordan is obviously referring to activism when amongst the features that characterise evangelicalism he writes:

> *Evangelicalism is a busy faith: Evangelicals are encouraged to live out their faith in detail of everyday life. A great deal of time is devoted to activities associated either with their local church or with a myriad of voluntary para-church organisations that have been established to express diversity of evangelical concerns.*[404]

Activism for the 2x2 movement is a mission held a few times a week during the winter months. All other meetings, Sunday fellowship, special meetings and conventions are for members only; from time to time an outsider may visit a convention but this is not encouraged. The movement shuns all community involvement and churches and other Christian organisations who are involved in community action. They treat the church like Noah's Ark that Skuce warns against, 'the local church is not Noah's Ark, keeping safe the few from the destructive world outside. Rather the church is the upper room, where the faith community has gathered, but cannot stay within as the love of Jesus points them outside.'[405]

The movement that claims that one can only find salvation through hearing the Gospel from one of their workers and then shows little interest in propagating the message amongst those who have never heard is something of a paradox. The current 2x2s stand in sharp contrast to those early workers who actively spread their message in missions that went on all year around and on town market days would be found preaching in the open air.

---

[403] McGrath, *Evangelicalism and the Future*, 73.
[404] Jordan, Glenn, *Not of this World*, (Belfast: Blackstaff Press, 2001), 19.
[405] Skuce, Stephen, *Faith Reborn*, (Calver: Cliff College Publishing, 2008), 98.

The activism that was the hallmark of classical evangelicalism was not only one of preaching the Gospel but one that reaches out to those in poverty and destitution. John Wesley's Methodism was passionately evangelistic but it also demonstrated the love of Christ. Wesley's letter to Wilberforce in support of the abolition of slavery shows his concern for the contemporary issues of his day. He writes, 'Go on, in the name of God and in the power of his might, till even American slavery (the vilest that ever saw the sun) shall vanish away before it.'[406] Commenting on the activism of evangelicalism in the nineteenth century, Bebbington writes, 'places of worship standardly maintained funds for the relief of the poor associated with their own congregations and many extended their philanthropy far wider.'[407]

The 2x2 movement simply avoids activities that could be construed as acts of mercy. They argue that within the fellowship they provide help and assistance for those in need. There is no involvement in the wider community or wider world. When I asked one established member about involvement in aid, she replied, 'on talking to a worker recently who labours in West Africa they said that their mission was to bring the bread of life to people. Acts 3 v 6 "Silver and gold have I none, but such as I have give thee."'[408]

Despite all their preaching on following the example of Jesus this is one area where they certainly do not emulate him, 'How God anointed Jesus of Nazareth with the Holy Ghost and with power: who went about doing good, and healing all that were oppressed of the devil; for God was with him' (Acts 10:38). It would be difficult to find any parallels between the activism that Bebbington defines and that of the 2x2 movement.

---

[406] Wesley, John, *The Works of John Wesley*, third edition, (Kansas: Beacon Hill Press, 1979), 153.

[407] Bebbington, *Dominance of Evangelicalism*, 36.

[408] Email 27th November 2011.

Theology Critique

The lack of a statement of beliefs make the critique of this movement's theology difficult but this research has been able to gather sufficient information to build a clear picture as to what they preach. I agree with Bray when he writes, 'Christian faith maintains the Bible is the normative, common witness of the spiritual truth which has been revealed to the Church. There is no other source comparable to this one, and no human authority can supersede or contradict it.'[409] Since the movement too claims support for what they believe this takes us to the important area of interpretation. Bray warns, 'individual believers must therefore test their experience in the light of common witness and submit to that.'[410]

Where does the 2x2 movement stand on the four pillars of evangelical Christianity: the Bible, the cross, conversion and activism?

The Bible

The 2x2 approach to the Bible is menu based in that they take from it what they need to support what they teach and leave the remainder unexplored. In my discussions, the sermons and emails from the apologists for the movement the same themes and texts arise. Essentially these are the texts that they believe give the command for an unsalaried, homeless ministry and the church that meets in the home.

Such apologists take an obscurantist stance and with tunnel vision are never prepared to consider the fact that Jesus did not leave a command for all time of an itinerant, homeless ministry and never once referred to the concept of the church meeting in the home. In the Bible, we find the doctrines of the Trinity, the divinity of Christ, the Gospel of grace alone through Christ alone, all of which the 2x2 movement is at best ambiguous about if not denying outright.

The doctrine of the Trinity is one of the cornerstones of the Christian

[409] Bray, *Biblical Interpretation*, 19.
[410] Bray, *Biblical Interpretation*, 15.

faith and failure to affirm it discards the very backbone of the Christian faith. Commenting on the Apostles' Creed Packer writes:

> *It is true that no explicit three-in-one formulations of God are found in surviving Christian literature until the third and fourth centuries. But is also true that the reality of the Father, the Son and the Holy Spirit working together as a team for the full salvation of sinners pervades the entire New Testament. It is not too much to say that the gospel, which tells of the Son coming to earth, dying to redeem us, sending the Spirit to us, and finally coming in judgement, all at the Father's will cannot be stated at all without speaking in an implicitly Trinitarian way.*[411]

The Cross

Workers will mention the blood of Christ in sermons and in prayers but as to exactly what they believe about the atonement, they are vague to the point of ambiguity. Cooper writes:

> *In all my years with this group I never heard the message of the Cross preached. I never heard how Christ died in my place and how that through one man, Adam, sin entered into the world and man was separated from God. I never heard how that through one man, Jesus Christ, man was reconciled to God through the shedding of His blood on the Cross. They do not point people to the Cross, but to them. They preach that Christ died only for them in their group, those who follow the workers, and not for the whole world.*[412]

From the large number of sermons I have heard at conventions and missions, not one has been on the Cross. For them it is a limited atonement, not in the Calvinist understanding, but for those within the 2x2 movement. Cooper's statement is an excellent summary of what the workers do not preach. Speaking at the Stockholm convention a senior Scottish Worker related a story of how as a young worker he was asked to visit the bedside of a dying man who at one time was part of the movement but no longer. Kerr said:

---

[411]   Packer, *Affirming the Apostles' Creed*, 19.
[412]   http://www.thelyingtruth.info/?f=noname&id=9.

And there were no workers available except me and I was fairly young at the time so I went and had a chat with the old fella and he was in absolute torment and I did not know what to say to him but I tried to talk to him about how he had wasted so much of his life but if his heart was right God could still do a work here. . . and I tried to encourage him as much as I could but I left him just in agony.[413]

As a listener I wondered, why did he not point him to the cross of Christ and explain the message of salvation? Had he used the story to illustrate that as an older and experienced worker what he would have done that would have been different but the story ended with no further comment.

Any Christian movement that neglects, rejects or minimises the centrality of Christ and his work on the cross abandons the right for inclusion in the evangelical Christian mainstream. The significance of the cross and the atonement is captured by Jeffery, Ovey and Sach: 'the doctrine of penal substitution states God gave himself in the person of his Son to suffer instead of us the death, punishment and curse due to fallen humanity as the penalty for sin. This understanding of the cross of Christ stands at the very heart of the gospel.'[414] Redemption is not the blood of Christ plus the homeless ministry and the church that meets in the home.

Conversion

Conversion is what the 2x2s refer to as 'professing'. For a movement that is pedantic about the use of words that reside in Scripture this term is not one found there in the strict context of conversion. This is an example of where terminology matters only if it is common currency within the movement. I have been unable to find at what stage the term professing entered the 2x2 terminology. Reading Trotter's account of the early days of the work he uses the word 'saved' to describe conversion – George Walker got saved, David Donaldson

---

[413] Bob Kerr speaking at Stockholm convention, July 2011.
[414] Jeffrey, Ovey and Sach, *Pierced For Our Transgressions*, 20.

got saved and he records the names of some who got saved at William Irvine's mission in Enniskillen Orange Hall in 1905. For the present day 2x2s 'professing' is more of a mental assent to indicate that one is following Jesus and becoming part of the movement. In retrospect, my grandmother's generation of the movement spoke more of their professing as an act of evangelical conversion and this identifies with Trotter's terminology. Over the years and throughout this research I have met many in the movement who testify to a living faith in Christ alone for their salvation. They do not represent the majority view who believes there is no salvation outside the movement and their ministry.

There are no calls to turn from sin, repent and find cleansing in the blood of Christ. The role of the worker must be to the forefront as is clear from Swanson who adds, 'we can always judge the state of a person's salvation by his attitude towards the Workers.'[415] This statement stands in total contrast to what the evidence of salvation is. It has nothing to do with the workers, it has to do with the centrality of Christ in the life of the believer and what God has done for them through Christ. According to Packer, 'New Testament salvation is the divine gift, to persons who know themselves to be godless and guilty, of a new relationship of reconciliation with God the creator through the mediatorial ministry of Jesus Christ the Saviour.'[416] Conversion in the evangelical sense is not part of the 2x2 teaching or doctrine and those who profess must show blind loyalty to a system that does not believe that Christ alone is sufficient for salvation.

---

[415] http://www.workersect.org/2x205g.html. Statement made by Everett Swanson a senior 2x2 worker in the US.
[416] Packer, J. I, *Celebrating the Saving Work of God*, (Carlisle: Paternoster Press, 1989), 52.

Activism and Social Action

History has many examples of men and women, some in full time Christian ministry, whose lives were spent in active service of the Gospel of Jesus Christ. There is no category in New Testament Christianity for silent or inactive witnesses. In John 15:16 we learn that Christians are chosen and appointed to bear fruit. Commenting on this verse Carson says, 'the fruit in short is new converts. One purpose of election, then, is that the disciples who have been so blessed with revelation and understanding, should win others to the faith. . . That is why the union of love that joins believers with Jesus can never become a comfortable, exclusivistic huddle that only they can share.'[417] This is one of the many injunctions to believers that are ignored by the 2x2 movement whose members do not witness openly to their faith. The main reason for this is that they believe that one can only come to faith if they hear the message from a worker. Since they believe that no other Christian denomination knows the truth of the Gospel, I have asked workers and members why they are not actively propagating this message to a world of lost sinners. Inane excuses follow, 'I invite people to gospel meetings'; 'the Spirit leads us where to go' and many others. When we see the activity of the first Christians in spreading their faith, we find no resemblance to the 2x2 movement.

A suitable role model for 2x2 workers is the apostle Paul and whilst there are countless examples of his activism, the most concise summary is his speech to the Ephesian elders in Acts 20: 17-36. Here is a summary of his work and his message - his teaching publicly and from house to house (v.20). The content of his message was 'repentance towards God and faith in our Lord Jesus Christ (v.21). His desire was to finish the course and 'the ministry I received from the Lord Jesus to testify to the gospel of the grace of God' (v.24). He declared the 'whole counsel of God' (v.27). How different all of this is from the preaching and lifestyle of the 2x2 workers. For Paul the gospel was a call to repentance and faith and the gospel of the grace of God. There was none of their emphasis on their patterns of ministry or the church in the home.

----

[417] Carson, D. A, *The Gospel According to John*, (Leicester: Apollos, 1991), 523.

His advice to the elders in v.28 is to care for themselves and for the flock where the Holy Spirit has made them overseers. The message that Paul preached had to be evident in the lives of the elders before they could look after the flock. The role of a true overseer is, 'to care for the Church of God which he obtained with his own blood'. Here is the emphasis on the importance of Christ's sacrifice at Calvary. Paul in his mission worked relentlessly for the spread of the gospel and worked to provide necessities for himself and others. Workers would do well to mirror Paul's industry and his message.

There is no evidence that this movement demonstrates a passion for the lost by engaging in evangelistic activity or ever shows evidence of their faith in Christ by works of compassion and mercy. In the history of the 2x2 movement to the present day, we do not find men or women with the evangelical fervour of some of those from generations past, whose active, living faith in Christ was shown by their works. There was Lord Shaftesbury with his campaign for the victims of an urban/industrial society; Thomas Guthrie, Edinburgh, was responsible for promoting a network of ragged schools similar to those backed by Shaftesbury; Spurgeon with his orphanage in Stockwell; Mueller's orphanages in Bristol and many others and there are numerous similar works today. These were all because of the outworking of the gospel. It is important to recognise that this social action did not replace the primary work of preaching the gospel but was in addition to it. 'It was a representative impulse to do good to the less fortunate members of society; a symptom of the large-hearted sense of mission that motivated the evangelicals of the Victorian era.'[418] The same should be true today but it is something that is a foreign concept to the 2x2 movement.

---

[418]   Bebbington, *Dominance of Evangelicalism*, (Leicester: Inter-Varsity Press, 2005), 36.

Conclusion

This is a complex movement, highly secretive in nature and extremely difficult to define because of the lack of continuity in their beliefs. They are entrenched in the notion that they alone represent the church that Jesus ordained during his earthly ministry. There are those within the membership who may take a more liberal approach and accept the validity of other Christian denominations; they do so silently and they are in a very small minority. They would not dare to speak openly of their convictions and if they did, it would mean excommunication. The movement brooks no dissent from its unwritten rules and beliefs and this absolutism instils fear into the membership and keeps them in line.

How else could such a religious movement, whose beliefs and rules lack an obvious rationale, get loyalty from members? Most members would prefer to ignore its history and give the erroneous impression that there is continuity with the New Testament church and that everything remains as it was then. A few passages of Scripture are used to justify the basis for the movement and to confirm the two main tenets of their system. These are the homeless ministry in same-sex pairs and the church that meets in the home. These are claimed to be the teaching of Jesus. In contrast, the New Testament writers make little reference to the teachings of Jesus. Dunn makes this point when he writes, 'Paul and the other letter writers in the New Testament show no interest whatsoever in the life of Jesus as such and bother to quote only a minimal handful of sayings spoken by Jesus during his earthly ministry.'[419]

The 2x2 overseers, workers and members have limited principles of interpretation and as a result find it easy to reach conclusions upon which they build doctrines and practices that lack a clear mandate from Scripture. Packer explains how this can happen when he writes, 'Scripture can only rule us as far as it is understood, and it is only understood so far as it is properly interpreted. A misinterpreted Bible

---

[419] Dunn, James D. G, *The Living Word*, 25.

is a misunderstood Bible, which will lead us out of God's way rather than in it. Interpretation must be right if biblical authority is to be real in our lives and in our churches.'[420]

The founders of the 2x2 movement built their doctrines on single obscure texts and over the years, followers have blindly emulated what was taught as revelation. They need to clear their minds of selected proof-texts and focus on what the Bible actually says.[421] It is little wonder that Hammond would state of those early preachers:

> *Most of the "Go Preachers" are men of limited knowledge of the doctrines of Christian faith, and as a result most extravagant utterances are traceable to them. Some of their preachers have contended that we are not saved by faith but imitating the life of Jesus as a man upon earth. Emphasis is laid on fidelity to the company rather than on personal lines, faith in the redeemer of men.*[422]

Hammond was in a strong position to assess the movement in that he entered the Church of Ireland ministry in Dublin in 1903 and served there until he moved to Australia in 1936 as principal of Moore College in Sydney. He was in Ireland during the formative years of the 2x2 movement and in Australia when they were still enjoying growth there.

The absence of any scholarly outline to support the doctrines and beliefs they espouse adds to the difficulty of giving any credibility to their claims. Their hermeneutic is limited to the framework of the homeless ministry and the church in the home and this has serious implications for the interpretation of Scripture. Dunn offers valuable guidance: 'an evangelical hermeneutic starts from the assumption that the New Testament attitude to, and use of, scripture provides a pattern for all subsequent Christian attitude to, and use of, scripture.'[423] Without a broader hermeneutical framework in place, interpretation of Scripture will be deeply flawed.

Throughout this research close observation of their modus operandi

---

[420] Packer, *Truth and Power*, 121.

[421] It is acknowledged that the same can be said of many Christian denominations.

[422] Hammond's statement was a short and succinct assessment of the movement prepared specifically for the New South Wales Council of Churches.

[423] Dunn, *Living Word*, 127

reveals the shape of a shapeless movement. For example, their doctrine of the church amounts to nothing more than the church that meets in the home and no alternative is countenanced. Because they take an obscurantist approach in such matters it is impossible to reason with them and one is reminded of the maxim, 'there are none so blind as those who will not see'. The nature of the church is important and Hanson offers reasoned thinking on the subject:

> There are two ways of regarding the origin of the Christian Church, both of them having some support in Scripture, and neither incompatible with the other. The first is to see the Church as a human institution founded by Jesus either when he praised Peter at Caesarea Philippi for acknowledging him as Christ (Matt. 16: 13-20) or when he breathed on the apostles after the resurrection (John 20; 19-23) or simply when he called the twelve apostles and gathered around him a band of disciples. There can be no doubt that this band of apostles and disciples constituted the continuing link between the days of the Lord's ministry in the flesh and the earliest days of the primitive Christian community after the resurrection. . . In the beginning the earliest apostles and disciples are the Church, not what we today would call the ministry, and if privileges are given or promises made to them these apply to the Church as a whole. . . The other way of regarding the foundation or origin of the Church is to be found in the letters written by Paul or attributed to him. Here no reference at all is made to Christ's foundation of the Church in the days of his flesh, but the Church springs out of the resurrection and the descent of the Spirit. The Church here is that community of people who are members of Christ's Body and who live in the Spirit.[424]

Hanson offers two explanations and both find validity in Scripture but a 2x2 member will not engage in such a discussion. On close examination of the Scriptures used to bolster the main tenets of the movement – the homeless preacher and the church in the home – neither has foundation. They restrict the Bible to the few texts that

----

[424] Hanson, A. T and Hanson, R. P. C, *Reasonable Faith*, (Oxford: Oxford University Press, 1981), 215.

support their ministry and fail to recognise the importance of the major doctrines of the Christian faith. These are the doctrine of the Trinity and the doctrine of the divinity of Christ, both of which they explicitly or implicitly reject. Everett Swanson's statement in 1969, 'Scripture is not the Word of God until it is spoken by a Worker,'[425] is the clearest evidence of a flawed view of Scripture as the Word of God.

Their view of the significance of the cross is best summed up from Stancliff's statement in 1980, (quoted earlier), 'my hope of salvation is the blood of Christ. But I would like to explain to you what it means. The blood of Christ is the ministry and the church in the home. Without the New Testament ministry you don't have the blood of Christ which includes the church in the home. The forgiveness of sins is a fringe benefit.'[426] This statement points to their exclusivity where the biblical doctrine of salvation is insufficient, unless accompanied by the 2x2 ministry and the church in the home.

Conversion as expressed in the Bible and 'professing' in the language of the 2x2s are not interchangeable. This is confirmed by Doug Parker, 'the doctrine of justification through faith alone in Jesus Christ as divine redeemer is contrary to the dogma of the nameless sect.'[427] The reductionist view of conversion preached by the 2x2 workers is not apparent in Scripture but is rather a syncretistic mix, partly contained in Scripture and added to by the workers. It holds no resemblance to the evangelical definition of conversion with its biblical grounding.

Activism is the last characteristic of Bebbington's quadrilateral and one with which the 2x2s show little or no interaction. Members will never make any effort to witness to their faith and when asked what they believe they are usually evasive and may possibly invite the enquirer to a gospel mission if there is one in the locality. This lack of openness and transparency leads to suspicion. One reason why they are reluctant to engage with outsiders on matters of faith is that they are imbued with the teaching that a person can only 'profess' through the medium of

---

[425] http://www.workersect.org/2x205g.html. Statement made Everett Swanson, a senior 2x2 worker in 1969.
[426] http://www.workersect.org/2x205g.html. Statement made by Leo Stancliff, a senior 2x2 worker at Sacramento, California, 1980.
[427] Parker, *Secret Sect*, 102.

a worker. Therefore, there is no point in a mere member witnessing unless the person can hear the message from a worker.

If this movement really believes that they are the only true form of Christianity then it would be reasonable to expect them to spread their message with zeal. Packer sums a Christian's responsibility up when he writes in the introduction to *The Reformed Pastor*:

> It is often said, quite fairly, that any Christian who seriously thinks that without Christ men are lost, and who seriously loves his neighbour, will not be able to rest for the thought that all around him people are going to hell, but will lay himself unstintingly to convert others as his prime task in life; and any Christian who fails so to live undermines the credibility of his faith, for if he cannot take it seriously as a guide for living, why should anyone else?[428]

For the 2x2 personal evangelism is not an option because they believe that only a worker can speak the gospel and lead a person to faith.

The term 'evangelical Christian' is irrelevant to the 2x2s, but this is the comparative criterion used throughout this research. In support of the importance of evangelical Christianity as defining terminology, Stott writes, 'we dare to claim that evangelical Christianity is original, apostolic, New Testament Christianity.'[429] This definition together with Bebbington's four characteristics of classical evangelicalism - the Bible, the cross, conversion and activism – the only conclusion, with the evidence before us, that the 2x2 movement falls short of earning the label of being evangelical.

An exclusive sect which claims to be Christian will usually affirm its commitment to the doctrines of the Christian faith but is exclusive because, for example, they have stringent conditions that must be met before membership, as is the case with the 2x2 movement.[430]

There is no doubt that the 2x2s fall under the umbrella of a New Religious Movement.[431] However, this is not part of the debate as this

---

[428] Baxter, Richard, *The Reformed Pastor*, (Edinburgh: Banner of Truth, 1974), 16.
[429] Stott, *Evangelical Truth*, 16.
[430] See comments on sects on page 19.
[431] See pages 17-20.

research limits itself to theological reflections. Because they reject the doctrines espoused by early Christian creeds and the characteristics of evangelicalism this study is concerned about outlining and understanding what those distinctives might be.

This research has established that this movement rejects the doctrines of the divinity of Christ, the Trinity and the significance of Christ's death on the cross as a sufficient sacrifice for redemption. Their emphasis is on the homeless preacher and the church that meets in the home, neither of which has a mandate in Scripture. The role of the worker is elevated to that of Jesus and the apostles and, by looking at the lives of the workers, people are expected to see an exact imprint of them. One worker preached this at a gospel mission:

> *I hope as you look at our lives that you can see two people [the two workers] spending their lives in exactly the same way that Jesus spent his life and that those early apostles spent their lives. I hope you don't see any different and that can be nothing that can confuse you. That as you can read our hearts, read our lives, that you can see an epistle clearly spoken that tells you what Jesus established many, many years ago still works today.*[432]

The view of those who have been workers and those who have had an opportunity to see the workers close up does not correspond to the content of their preaching. The gospel preached by the 2x2s is reduced to following the example of Jesus, the church that meets in the home and the homeless preacher. The 2x2s demonstrate enough to let them pass as a quaint and primitive Christian movement wishing to emulate that of the New Testament believers, but at the same time reject the uniqueness of the Gospel of Jesus Christ as accepted by evangelical Christianity as historical, rational and empirical.

Their exclusivity initially leads to the thinking that the movement may simply exhibit cult tendencies but closer investigation reveals that they reject doctrines that are central to the Christian faith. Having examined the movement under the spotlight of the four characteristics of classical evangelicalism – the Bible, the cross, conversion and

---

[432] Edgar Lowe preaching at a mission in Richhill, County Armagh, 21st November 2011.

activism – they fail to meet the criteria on every single one. On the road towards a conclusion, there has been reflection on the definitions of a cult from a theological perspective.

Unfortunately, cult is often a designation given to a movement simply because of a personal disagreement with its beliefs and practices or sometimes used pejoratively. In this research, it is used within the context of the accepted definitions of cults of Christianity. There are several definitions and these are all broadly similar to that of Enroth.[433] Sire writes that a cult is, 'Any religious movement that is organizationally distinct and has doctrines and/or practices that contradict those of the Scriptures as interpreted by traditional Christianity as represented by major Catholic and Protestant denominations, and as expressed in such statements as the Apostles' Creed.'[434]

One simple and important definition of a cult of Christianity is, 'therefore for orthodox Christianity, cults of Christianity are groups that while claiming to be Christian deny central doctrinal tenets such as the Trinity and the deity of Jesus Christ. They deviate from the doctrinal norms set forth in the Bible and historical creeds of Christendom.'[435] This research has shown that the movement rejects central doctrines such as the Trinity, the deity of Christ and could not affirm the historical creeds. Therefore, the only reasonable conclusion one can reach is that the 2x2 movement is a cult and a particularly dangerous one.

---

[433] See page 19.
[434] Sire, James, *Scripture Twisting: 20 Ways Cults Misread the Bible*, (Downers Grove: IVP, 1980), 20.
[435] Mather, Nichols and Schmidt, *Encyclopedic Dictionary of Cults, Sects and World Religions*, 381.

Appendices

Appendix 1

Terminology

To clarify the terms used in this research it is important to give a brief explanation and definition of the some of the terms used within the 2x2s. A more detailed explanation of the full range of terminology is available in Lloyd Fortt's book, *A Search for "the Truth"*[436].

Friend	only those people professing [within] the faith.
Worker	a Preacher who does the work of preaching the gospel and officiates at funerals but not at weddings.
Saint	same as friend
Profess	the act of declaration in a gospel mission that the person wishes to follow the beliefs and practices of the 2x2s.
Outsider	any person not a member or professing
Preparation	the act of volunteer work at any convention centre whereby members give days of their time helping to prepare meeting, eating and sleeping facilities at the site.
Mission	holding of gospel meetings for the purpose of winning new converts
Truth	the entire beliefs and practices of the 2x2s as they view all other Christians as totally misguided and living a lie.
Resting	this is when a worker takes time out due to factors such as illness, stress and is not assigned to a preaching rota.

....

[436] Fortt, Lloyd, *A Search for "the Truth"*, (Bend: Research and Information Services, 1994).

Appendix 2

Following the publication of *The Secret Sect* newspaper reporters in the US for the first time took an active interest in the 2x2 conventions visiting the grounds, speaking with members and workers. These extracts of the news reports and my comments indicate how ignorant those outside Ireland were of the origins of the movement.

This meant a wave of publicity that for a brief time placed the convention, workers and friends and their beliefs in the public limelight. An editorial published in the *Walla Walla Union Bulletin* on 11th June 1982 brought two Washington conventions out of their seclusion. Their anonymity began to erode and this brought mixed reactions as shown by the following excerpts[437]:

The reporter visiting the Miltown convention questioned the group's origins: 'When one participant was asked when the fellowship began, he referred to the time of Christ'. (June 11, 1982, *Walla Walla Union Bulletin*)[438]

Speaking to the Los Angeles Times, (Sept. 13, 1983), worker-spokesman, David Kennedy agreed, 'friends would probably tell you this fellowship began with Christ.'[439] Several publications, *The Spokesman Review, Skagit Valley Herald, Post Falls* and *Bellingham Herald* carried the following comments:

> *Doug and Helen Parker's book, The Secret Sect made its public debut in the United States in some newspaper articles printed while two large conventions were taking place in Washington and Idaho, simultaneously. The conventions were held at Post Falls and Bonners Ferry, Idaho; and Walla Walla and Chelan, Washington; and the week after, at Miltown in Southeast Washington.*[440]

[437] http://www.tellingthetruth.info/founder_book/27wmibook.php#SECRETSECT. Accessed 21 August 2011.
[438] http://www.tellingthetruth.info/founder_book/27wmibook.php#SECRETSECT. Accessed 21 August 2011.
[439] http://www.tellingthetruth.info/founder_book/27wmibook.php#SECRETSECT. Accessed 21 August 2011.
[440] http://www.tellingthetruth.info/founder_book/27wmibook.php#SECRETSECT. Accessed 21 August 2011.

A string of newspaper articles printed in 1983 published the views of a number of 2x2 members and workers, as well as those of former members.

> *Several former members said they had been led to believe the group went back to the time of Christ. They said, 'We're the original church. We follow the Jesus Way,' one ex-member recalled. Several former members report that discovering otherwise was the key blow to their faith in the Two by Twos. They point to a book that traced the group back only as far as 1897, to a movement founded in Ireland by William Irvine. (June 5, 1983, Spokesman Review)*

> *The origins of the church are another source of criticism say ex-members. Ex-members contend they were led to believe the church is the continuation of the New Testament church, begun at the time of Christ's death. An 11-year-old member, David Woods of Saint Helens, Ore., described his church this way during last year's convention: 'If you want to get the right way you have to get the oldest...the best church is the oldest church, and this is the oldest church because this church began when the first person was born.' (August 17, 198, Skagit Valley Herald)*

As I have spoken with members, young and old, this comment by an eleven-year-old personifies the brainwashing that those born into the movement get from a very young age. They may not be politically dangerous or resort to kidnapping but certainly there is a strong element of brainwashing. I have spoken to those now in their fifties and sixties who were born into the movement but who never made a profession and have no other church connections. They still believe that the 2x2 movement is the only true way to God. From the following excerpts,[441] we can see the reaction when reporters in the US attended conventions with workers on hand to defend the movement's history:

> *Walter Pollock, a 'worker' or minister, said he was disappointed to learn the Spokane articles were published simultaneously with an advertisement for a book by ex-member Doug Parker, The Secret Sect, a historical account of the group's origins and an exploration*

---

[441] http://www.tellingthetruth.info/founder_book/27wmibook.php#SECRETSECT. Accessed 21 August 2011.

of its theological positions that members consider unflattering. Mike Archhowld, The Spokesman reviews assistant city editor, denied any collaboration between the editorial and advertising departments on the story. (August 17, 1983, Skagit Valley Herald)

Parker last year published his findings in The Secret Sect, a book available at area bookstores. The book and the publicity about the group that has followed its publication, threatens a crisis within the group that may alter it forever, says Johnson of the University of Oregon...Parker charges leaders have worked since the early 1930s to conceal the group's origins, substituting a version more to their liking. (August 20, 1983, Bellingham Herald Saturday)

However, according to author and ex-member Doug Parker, the church actually was founded in 1897 by William Irvine in Ireland. Irvine was joined in 1901 by Edward Cooney, who assisted in leadership organization until his excommunication in 1928. When Parker's book 'The Secret Sect' first appeared, workers denied his historical account of the group's origins, say ex-members. Now they say the ministers are 'whitewashing' the revelation, saying it isn't significant. (August 17, 1983, Skagit Valley Herald).

A number of workers jumped to the defence of the movement's stance with the following response:

Pollock said he doesn't understand why the question of the group's history should be traumatic for ex-members. 'I don't know how they could have come up with that,' said Pollock, who denied that the fellowship makes unsubstantiated claims about its origins. 'We know that it began with a group of men in the British Isles around the turn of the century. That's as far as we've been able to trace it.'

Sylvester, [Therald] responding to Parker's charges, says deciding which version is the truth is unimportant. 'Jesus himself set us up,' he said. 'Whether it was planted in the first century, the 10th century or the 20th century, the message is the same, it produces the same thing. They say we're a secret thing. But anyone that has the Bible has the way. People spread wrong reports about us. They spread wrong reports about Jesus. Prejudiced and bitter people will tell you things that are not true'. (August 20 1983, Bellingham Herald)

'We don't deny that,' said Therald Sylvester, Washington overseer, when asked if the historical account was true. He refused, however, to discuss why ex-members had a different impression. 'I won't go into that detail,' he said. (August 20 1983 Bellingham Herald)

Richard Wulf, 27, a Two-by-Two worker in Mexico for two years, was asked about this apparent suppression of the sect's origins. 'Near the turn of the century God raised up godly men in Ireland and Scotland,' Wulf acknowledged. 'We respect them and what they established. But we don't hold to that history and line of succession.' Added (David) Kennedy: 'Now we're not following these men but the New Testament. What we have today is the New Testament fellowship.' (Sept. 13, 1983. Los Angeles Times)[442]

Appendix 3

Extracts from *Bright Words*, the official magazine of the Faith Mission chart Irvine's time with the movement including and following his resignation.

Reports that appeared in the *Bright Words* magazine would indicate that Irvine was an active and popular worker for the mission:

NENAGH — Eight months ago, before the advent of the Faith Mission, it would have been almost impossible to "unearth" more than a dozen live Christians in this town ... When Pilgrim Irvine arrived here last August, he found the spiritual light of the place burning dimly. However, before he closed a six weeks' mission, several backsliders were restored, and a number of souls had yielded to the Holy Spirit's pleading, and are now rejoicing in the excellency of the knowledge of Christ Jesus. . .Pilgrims Pendreigh and McLean have just closed a sixteen days' mission in connection with our Prayer Union. Pilgrims Irvine and Hughes came over from Borisokane for the occasion. All present were delighted to see our two brothers again. The first-named delivered a very telling and suitable address, and the latter gave us a few words of encouragement, which were appreciated by all his Nenagh friends.

---

[442] http://www.tellingthetruth.info/founder_book/27wmibook.php#SECRETSECT. Accessed 21 August 2011.

The meeting was then left open for testimonies, each one telling what the Lord had done for them, and several praising God for the Faith Mission, and for Pilgrim Irvine in particular, and also for sending the sisters to Nenagh.[443]

Irvine's dedication to the work of the Faith Mission was soon to change and from March 1900, *Bright Words* reports indicate that all was not well with Irvine's relationship with the Faith Mission. There had been a change in Irvine's activities well before that date. *Bright Words* records:

Pilgrim Irvine is in the south of Ireland. We have not had regular reports from him lately, but he has been building two movable wooden Halls, and has also had meetings at Cloughjordan, Roscrea, Moneygall, Kildare, and other places, attended with a good deal of blessing. The wooden halls are cheaply put up, and he writes of them as a great success, proposing that we should have some for Scottish counties. This we will consider. The friends at Rathmolyon, County Meath, are also building one to be used in that county.[444]

In *Bright Words* August 1901 Irvine's name has disappeared from the list of pilgrim workers and Govan makes a report of a visit to Ireland, 'a number of young people are going out on quite independent lines holding missions in various parts both of Ireland and Scotland. . . as some have been mistaken for pilgrims, we think it necessary to say that the Faith Mission is not responsible for this movement'.[445] This was an obvious reference to Irvine's new movement. He did not resign from the Faith Mission until 1901 and in September 1901 *Bright Words* make a brief reference to Irvine indicating that he had broken ties with the mission: "During the year several have dropped out from our LIST OF WORKERS. Pilgrim Irvine has been working on independent lines, chiefly in Ireland. Then quite recently Pilgrim Kelly has resigned, and also allied himself to these independent workers".[446] There continued to be some confusion regarding Irvine's status and his links to the Faith Mission and in May 1903, it was necessary for *Bright Words* to carry the following statement of clarification:

---

[443] *Bright Words* 15th April 1898, 91-92.
[444] *Bright Words* March 1900, 56-57.
[445] *Bright Words*, August 1901, 175-176.
[446] *Bright Words*, September 1901, 212.

...We regret that it seems needful, owing to confusing statements that have been made to state plainly that we have no responsibility for the work carried on in Ireland and elsewhere by Mr. Irvine and his fellow-workers. Having little organisation or arrangement whereby to distinguish them, the agents of this anonymous work have in some places been mistaken for our Faith Mission pilgrims, and misleading references have in consequence appeared in the public press. [447]

This report and further reports in *Bright Words* claimed that the Faith Mission was being misrepresented and felt it necessary to issue statements disassociating themselves from the work of Irvine and his followers:

We regret that it seems necessary to again point out that missions are being held in various parts by persons who represent themselves to be "Faith Mission" workers, but who are not in any way under our control or direction. This movement which has almost no organisation and little method, was started by Mr. Wm. Irvine, at one time much used as a pilgrim in our Mission, and some of whose converts we are glad to have as efficient workers among us today. Though somewhat on our lines there are various points, both in method and teaching, that we do not approve of, and in which they widely differ from us. Then we hear of instances in which some of these irresponsible workers have misrepresented and spoken against the Faith Mission, while taking personal advantage of it by holding missions in places we have already worked, and seeking the support of our Prayer Unions. [448]

---

[447]   *Bright Words*, May 1903, 102.
[448]   *Bright Words*, December 1903, 27.

Appendix 4

Extract of the transcript of Herbie Jennings' sermon:

You have heard this before and you're tired listening to me but I came here, one time . . . to this (sic) very grounds. I remember this platform, it was a different one I'm sure, I remember that door. . . I asked God to convict, I asked that. . . I didn't want to go do the work, I didn't want to do this preaching of the gospel, it didn't suit me, it didn't suit my nature, but I was afflicted to do it for years. And it was getting to the stage now I was going to lose my peace so I had do something. I prayed earnestly that I would come here that the workers, visiting workers, would give their testimony, about the work. And it happened in the first meeting and happened in the second and happened in the third meeting, you know this is no coincidence, God does hear prayer, God will answer prayer it's God's doings. It was an impossibility for anybody to know the vow that I had made, you know I'm drawing attention to myself, that's not the point. . . I prayed that it would happen in those meetings and I remember speaking on Sunday morning and I do remember what I spoke on. Standing over there and by the way at this convention this particular meeting, I said I must make it known that now I promised God that I would make it known that the work is my place, if He made known to me that the work is my place I promised God that I would take that step and that direction, so I wanted to make it known. After five meetings I couldn't stick it any longer, I had to make it known. Because in every meeting all visitors spoke about the work and their experience, I remember certain people, Gordon Anderson was here, Luke Kennan was here, Irvine Pearson was here, others as well. And I remember going out of that door there after second meeting on Sunday waiting for him there, when he came I couldn't tell him what was on my mind. So he put his arm on my shoulder and we walked along there and he said are you trying to tell me, are you telling me that you want to go into this work, I said yes. So walked he walked across with me and tried to tell him a little bit of his own experience and so on. So together, I had to go on, I had to go. But I didn't realize I still remember I was sitting in here, down there in the next meeting and uncle Irvine [Pearson]stood up here to speak, I didn't know he speaking and he said I'm going to say something, he said I've been trying to get away from it, but he I've nothing else to tell you. And he gave his own experience about going to work. . . It was very easy, it wasn't easy for him to speak and it wasn't easy for some of us to listen either. But it was just a real experience, I'm only mentioning this because you know, this work is of God, this thing is of God. No other way would this happen, it's God's doing, it's God's doings. Real confirmation, ah and, other workers here, both sides [male and female] they can tell you the same thing, conviction, you ask for it, and God will give it to you and God will show you what He has in mind for your life and it's a good future when God is in it.[449]

---

[449] Cork Convention, Saturday morning June 2010

Appendix 5

On pages 170 and 171 is a JPG of the statement prepared and printed by Archdeacon T C Hammond, *Cooneyites and Go-Preachers* for the New South Wales Council of Churches in 1955.

The following statement was prepared by Archdeacon T. C. Hammond, and is printed for the New South Wales Council of Churches.

In various parts of Australia, as in other parts of the world, a group of preachers is operating and causing deep concern to the clergy and people in many churches, particularly in the areas where they hold their meetings.

At first sight there seems to be little that is unusual about them. They have no name and are at great pains to emphasise the fact that they have NO NAME. To outward appearance they seem to have no "peculiar" doctrines or practices, for they claim to be sincere followers of Jesus Christ, and set themselves up as Gospel preachers.

Closer examination and investigation, however, reveals that for certain official purposes they are registered under the name of "The United Christian Conventions of Australia and New Zealand," and that they also go by the name of "The Testimony of Jesus" or followers of "the Jesus Way." Two other titles which may be attached to them are, "Go Preachers" and "Cooney-ites."

They claim to be the only company of believers in our Lord Jesus Christ who observe the conditions laid down in the New Testament for the guidance of disciples.

They are very hostile to all who do not subscribe to their peculiar tenets, and are particularly virulent in their denunciations of all ministers of religion.

The origin of this particular body can be traced to the activ-

ities of William Irvine and Edward Cooney.

William Irvine was a native of Kilsyth, in Scotland. He was converted through the influence of the Rev. John McNeil, a Presbyterian minister who, after occupying the pulpit of Regents Park Church, in London, devoted himself with remarkable success to the work of evangelism.

Shortly after his conversion, William Irvine joined the Faith Mission, an evangelistic organisation connected with the name of John Govan. The Faith Mission was an interdenominational society which worked in cordial co-operation with the existing churches, and directed converts who were impressed at the meetings held by them, to associate themselves with the congregation to which they belonged. It is scarcely necessary to add that the Rev. John McNeil adopted the same principle.

The danger which accompanies all such movements, and which is not confined to them, but is often manifested in deep religious movements within the strict limits of denominational activities, is that earnest, but not well-balanced, souls may be caught up in the enthusiasm engendered by earnest appeals, and may lay undue emphasis on personal experience to the loss of sound scriptural knowledge.

Evidently William Irvine had a mystical and rather excitable temperament. He was apt to regard his personal actions as determinent of truth regardless of the Gospel, inasmuch as towards the close of his life he took up his abode in Jerusalem, believing that he was the witness mentioned in the book of Revelation whose body will lie three and a half days in the streets of Jerusalem.

The movement inaugurated by him and greatly furthered by the enthusiasm of Mr. Edward Cooney, a native of Enniskillen, Co. Fermanagh, Ireland, unfortunately withdrew from all association with other religious bodies. They divided their adherents into two classes—the "Go Preachers," who are required to abandon all means of livelihood and live on the free will offerings of the disciples, and the ordinary members, who are invited to give generously for the support of the "Go Preachers."

The advocates of this body contend that the injunctions in Matthew 10 are directed for the whole of Christ's followers, and for all time. They ignore the command, "Go not into the way of the Gentiles and into any city of the Samaritans enter ye not," which plainly indicates the temporary nature of this particular commission to the twelve.

Unfortunately the requirement made that "Go Preachers" should deposit all their worldly possessions in a central fund, and go out without even shoes or two coats, has led to the unhappy divisions in families and amongst the adherents of "The United Christian Conventions."

It is only natural that those who have hastily committed themselves to a rash enterprise and afterwards regretted their action, should be disposed to question the absolute sincerity of those who invited them to make a rash venture. The inner divisions, consequent upon incidents such as these, has led to even Mr. Edward Cooney himself being visited with a measure of displeasure, amounting almost, if not altogether, to excommunication.

Christian homes have been divided, and much internal dissention created in various Christian congregations through the activity of these persons, and particularly through their antagonistic attitude towards all other professing Christians. Not only are the members of the ministry denounced, but the practice of attending Sunday School and the habit of church attendance have come under the severest censure.

Most of the "Go Preachers" are men of limited knowledge of the doctrines of the Christian faith, and as a result most extravagant utterances are traceable to them. Some of their preachers have contended that we are not saved by faith, but by imitating the life of Jesus as a man upon earth. Emphasis is laid on the fidelity to the company rather than on personal lines, faith in the Redeemer of men.

They seem to have adopted, in an exaggerated form, the old opinion of an inner illumination and regard the Bible apart from the interpretation of their experiences as simply a dead book. The discouragement of marriage amongst the preachers, and the separation of husband and wife in their preaching ministry, where marriage has taken place before the call to become a "Go Preacher," are potent of many possible evils, as the history of enforced celibacy abundantly proves.

In view of the grave consequences that have followed the entry of these missionaries into the various districts, the Council of Churches feels that it ought to address this warning to the ministers of denominations afflicted with it.

171

Bibliography

Acheson, Alan, Dublin, *A History of the Church of Ireland 1691 – 2001*, 2nd Edition, Columba Press, 2002

Aland, Kurt, *A History of Christianity*, Philadelphia, Fortress Press, English Translation. 1985

Allison, Gregg R, *Historical Theology*, Grand Rapids, Zondervan, 2011

Bailey, Kenneth E, *Jesus, Through Middle Eastern Eyes*, London: SPCK, 2008

Bailey, Kenneth, *Paul, Through Mediterranean Eyes*, London: SPCK, 2011

Baker Warren, editor, *Strong's Complete Word Study Concordance*, Chattanooga: AMG Publishers, 2004

Ballinamallard - A Place of Importance, (Published by the Ballinamallard Historical Society),

Barnett, Paul, *The Birth of Christianity*, Grand Rapids, Eerdmans, 2005

Barclay, William, *New Testament Words*, London: SCM, 2000

Baxter, Richard, *The Reformed Pastor*, Edinburgh: Banner of Truth, 1974

Bebbington, D. W, *Evangelicalism in Modern Britain*, London, Unwin Hyman, 1989

Bebbington, David W, *The Dominance of Evangelicalism*, Leicester: IVP, 2005.

Blaise, Antony J, Turcotte, Paul-Andre and Duhaime, Jean, editors, *Handbook of Early Christianity*, Oxford: AltaMira Press, 2002

Blomberg, Craig L, *Jesus and the Gospels*, Leicester, Apollos, 1997

Blomberg, Craig L, *Contagious Holiness*, Leicester, IVP, 2005

Bray, Gerald, *Creeds, Councils and Christ*, Leicester: IVP, 1984

Bray, Gerald, *Biblical Interpretation: Past and Present*, Downers Grove: IVP, 1996

Bruce, F. F. *The Spreading Flame*, Volume 1, Exeter, Paternoster, 1958

Bruce, Steve, *Religion in the Modern World*, Oxford: Oxford University Press, 1996.

Caird, G. B. *The Apostolic Age*, London, Duckworth, 1955

Carson, D. A and Woodbridge, John D, editors, *Hermeneutics, Authority and Canon*, Grand Rapids: Baker Books, 1985

Carson, D. A, *The Gospel According to John*, Leicester: Apollos, 1991

Chadwick, Henry, *The Early Church*, London: Penguin Books, 1993

Chandler, Matt, *The Explicit Gospel*, Nottingham: IVP, 2012

Chapman Daurelle, Editor, *Reflections*, Oregon, Research and Information Services, 1993

Chester, Tim, *A Meal with Jesus*, Nottingham: IVP, 2011

Chryssides, George D, *Exploring New Religions*, London, Continuum, 2001

Coalter, George J, *My Memoirs 1890 – 1950*, Enniskillen: William Trimble, 1951

Cooper, Lynn, *The Church With No Name*, published in 1996 and available online: http://www.thelyingtruth.info/?f=noname&id=2

Cole, R. Alan, *Mark*, 2nd edition, Leicester: IVP, 1989

Croft, Steven, editor, *Mission-shaped Questions*, London: Church House Publishing, 2008

Cross, F.L and Livingstone, E.A. *The Oxford Dictionary of the Christian Church*, 3rd edition revised. Oxford, Oxford University Press, 2005

Crow, Keith W. *THE INVISIBLE CHURCH*, A THESIS, Presented to the Department of Sociology and the Graduate School of the University of Oregon in partial fulfilment of the requirements for the degree of Master of Arts March 1961

Daniel, Joan F. Editor, *Reflected Truth*, Oregon, Research and Information Services, 1996

Daniel, Kevin N, *Reinventing the Truth*, Oregon, Research and Information Services, 1993

Driscoll, Mark and Breshears, Gerry, *Vintage Church*, Wheaton: Crossway Books, 2008

Dunn, James D. G, *Unity and Diversity in the New Testament*, London: SCM Press, 1977

Dunn, James, D. G, *The Living Word*, London, SCM Press, 1987

Ferguson, Sinclair B and Wright David F, editors, *New Dictionary of Theology*, Leicester: IVP, 1988

Fortt, Lloyd, *A Search for "the Truth"*, Oregon, Research and Information Services, 1994

Foster, Paul, editor, *The Writings of the Apostolic Fathers*, London: T&T Clark, 2007

France, R.T, *Matthew*, (Leicester: IVP, 1985

Frend, W.H.C, *The Early Church*, 3rd edition, London: SCM Press, 2003

Govan, I.R, *Spirit of Revival*, Edinburgh, Faith Mission Publish Department, 1938

Hall, Stuart G, *Doctrine and Practice in the Early Church*, London, SPCK, 1991

Hanson, A. T and Hanson, R. P. C, *Reasonable Faith*, Oxford: Oxford University Press, 1981

Helm, Paul and Trueman, Carl, editors, *The Trustworthiness of God*, Leicester, Apollos, 2002

Henry, Carl F.H, editor, *Revelation And The Bible*, London: Tyndale Press, 1959

Hinnells, John, editor, *The Routledge companion to the study of religion*, Abingdon: Routledge, 2005

Horton, Michael, *The Gospel-Driven Life*, (Grand Rapids: Baker Books, 2009),

Jaenen, Cornelius J, *The Apostles' Doctrine and Fellowship*, Ottawa: Legas, 2003

Jeffrey, Steve, Ovey, Mike and Sach, Andrew, *Pierced for our Transgressions*, Nottingham: IVP, 2007

Jordan, Glenn, *Not of this World*, Belfast: Blackstaff Press, 2001

Kantzer, Kenneth S. & Henry, Carl E. H, editors, *Evangelical Affirmations*, Grand Rapids: Zondervan, 1990

Klein, William W, Blomberg, Craig L and Hubbard, Robert L, *Introduction to Biblical Interpretation*, Nashville: Thomas Nelson, 1993

Köstenberger, Andreas, Kellum, L Scott. and Quarles, Charles L, *The Cradle, The Cross and The Crown*, Nashville: B&H Publishing, 2009

Legge, David, *Strongholds Shaken*, Belfast, Ambassador International, 2007

MacCulloch, Diarmaid, *Christianity: The First Three Thousand Years*, New York: Viking, 2010

McArthur, John F, Jr. *Charismatic Chaos*, (Grand Rapids: Zondervan, 1992

McDermott, Gerald R, *Can Evangelicals Learn from World Religions*, Downers Grove: IVP, 2003

McGavran, Donald A, *Understanding Church Growth*, 3rd edition revised and edited Wagner, Peter C, Grand Rapids, Eerdmans, 1991

McGrath, Alister, *To Know and to Serve God*, London, Hodder and Stoughton, 1977

McGrath, Alister, *Evangelicalism and the Future of Christianity*, London: Hodder and Stoughton, 1993

McGrath, Alister E, *Christian Theology*, 4th Edition, Oxford, Blackwell, 2007

Mather, George A, Nichols, Larry A, and Schmidt, Alvin J, editors, *Encylopedic Dictionary of Cults, Sects and World Religions*, Grand Rapids, Zondervan, 1993

Morris, Leon, *Luke*, Nottingham: IVP, 1988

Noll, Mark A, *The Scandal of the Evangelical Mind*, Leicester: IVP, 1994

Noll, Mark A, *The Rise of Evangelicalism*, Leicester, IVP, 2004

Packer, J I, *The Evangelical Anglican Identity Problem: An Analysis*, Oxford: Latimer House, 1978

Packer, J I, *Celebrating the Saving Work of God*, Carlisle: Paternoster Press, 1989

Packer, J I, *Truth and Power*, Guildford, Eagle Publishing, 1996

Packer, J I, *Faithfulness and Holiness*, Wheaton: Crossway, 2002

Packer, J I, *Affirming the Apostles' Creed*, Wheaton: Crossway, 2008

Parker, Doug and Helen, *The Secret Sect*, Sydney: Macarthur Press (Books) Pty. Ltd., 1982

Quick, Jon E, *Odyssey of a Soul in Bondage*, Oregon, Research and Information Services, 2007

Roberts, Patricia, *The Life and Ministry of Edward Cooney*, Enniskillen, William Trimble Ltd. 1991

Roberts, Patricia, *Selected Letters Hymns and Poems of Edward Cooney*, Enniskillen, William Trimble Ltd. 1990

Roberts, Patricia, *The Go Preacher Movement An Anthology*, Enniskillen, William Trimble Ltd. 2000

Saliba, John, A, *Perspectives on New Religious Movements*, London: Chapman, 1995

Sanders, E P, *Paul, the Law and the Jewish People*, London: SCM Press, 1985

Sire, James, *Scripture Twisting: 20 Ways Cults Misread the Bible*, Downers Grove: IVP, 1980

Skuce, Stephen, *Faith Reborn*, Calver: Cliff College Publishing, 2008

Steer, Roger, *Guarding the Holy Fire*, Grand Rapids, Baker, 1999

Stevenson, J. Revised by Frend, W.H.C, *A New Eusebius*, revised edition, London: SPCK, 1987

Stone, David, *The Church Without a Name*, no publisher or date listed

Stott, John, *Our Guilty Silence*, Leicester, IVP, 1967

Stott, John R. W, *The Message of Acts*, 2nd edition, Leicester: IVP, 1991

Stott, John, *Evangelical Truth*, Leicester, IVP, 2003

Stott, John, *The Living Church*, Nottingham, IVP, 2007

Stackhouse, John G, Editor, *No other Gods before Me*, Grand Rapids: Baker Academic, 2001

Telford, John, *The Life of John Wesley*, second edition, Belfast: Ambassador Publications, 1999

Thompson, Mark D, *Saving the Heart*, Kingsford: Matthias Media, 1995

Thompson, Mark D, *A Clear and Present Word*, Nottingham: Apollos, 2006

Tidball, Derek J, *Who are the Evangelicals*, London, Marshall Pickering, 1994

Tidball, Derek, *Ministry by the Book*, Nottingham, Apollos, 2008

Underwood, A.C, *A History of the English Baptists*, (London: Carey Kingsgate Press, 1947

Viola, Frank and Barna, George, *Pagan Christianity*, Barna, 2007

Wesley, John, *The Works of John Wesley*, third edition, Kansas: Beacon Hill Press, 1979

Zacharias, Ravi, editor, *Beyond Opinion*, Nashville: Thomas Nelson, 2007

All Bible quotations are from the King James Version unless otherwise identified.

ABBREVIATIONS

ESV   English Standard Version, London, Collins, 2002.

KJV   King James Version, London: Oxford University Press

NIV   New International Version, Grand Rapids, Zondervan, 1985.

RSV   Revised Standard Version, Nashville, Nelson, 1973.

Websites

www.census.nationalarchives.ie. http://www.census.nationalarchives.
ie/pages/1901/Fermanagh/Ballydoolagh/Mullaghmeen/1363719/.

http://www.census.nationalarchives.ie/pages/1901/Fermanagh/
Monea/Leighan/1362544/.

http://www.tellingthetruth.info/founder_book/27wmibook.
php#SECRETSECT. :

http://www.thisismoney.co.uk/money/bills/article-1633409/
Historic-inflation-calculator-value-money-changed-1900.html.

http://www.tellingthetruth.info/publications_johnlong/index.php.

http://www.tellingthetruth.info/workers_articles/marriageb.
php#February12.

http://www.votisalive.com/content/paul-sharp-funeral-false-church-
christian-life-assembly-circa-11-1-11.

http://professing.proboards.com/index.cgi?action=display&board=g
eneral&thread=18520&page=1.

http://www.anotherstep.net/ourstory/.

http://www.michigansthumb.com/articles/2010/02/09/news/
police_-_courts/doc4b715c17bc564579368752.txt.

http://www.wingsfortruth.info/noeltanner.pdf.

http://www.wingsfortruth.info/robertkee.pdf.

http://www.trutharchive.net/doug-morse---the-holy-spirit---2nd-
pilerwa-australia---2011.

http://professing.proboards.com/index.cgi?board=general&action=
display&thread=18845&page=1.

http://www.workersect.org/2x205g.html.

http://professing.proboards.com/index.cgi?board=general&action=
display&thread=18802&page=2.

http://multitext.ucc.ie/d/Ireland_religion__culture_1870-1914.

http://www.thelyingtruth.info/?f=noname&id=9.

http://www.workersect.org/2x205g.html.

http://www.votisalive.com/content/worldwide-convention-list-2008-here-accurate-count-2x2-conventions.

http://dialogueireland.wordpress.com/2012/02/08/two-by-twos-by-someone-who-grew-up-and-out-of-the-movement/#comment-15446.

http://www.tellingthetruth.info/plogger/?level=picture&id=293.

Journals and Magazines

Bright Words, the quarterly magazine and is the official organ of the Faith Mission, Edinburgh.

Impartial Reporter, a weekly provincial newspaper covering County Fermanagh and published weekly by William Trimble Limited.

Hammond Report was delivered by T C Hammond to the New South Wales Council of Churches in 1955 entitled, 'Cooneyites and Go-Preachers'.

Missiology, Vol. XXXII (1), 1985, 5-21

Epilogue

Throughout my research I met many wonderful people in the 2x2 movement. From my discussions I believe there are those who have a genuine, living faith in Christ alone for their salvation. For the majority of 'professing people' that I met I could only think of the answer given by the Lord Jesus Christ: 'you are not far from the kingdom of God' (Mark 12:34). But as we read the Scriptures we quickly learn that being 'not far' from the kingdom of God will not save us or prepare us for heaven.

The early workers in the 2x2 movement talked of being 'saved', but this changed to the talk of 'professing'. That this is neither a trivial phenomenon nor a petty quibbling-point can easily be seen in the light of an examination as to why this shift has occurred. The implications behind the two words illustrate well my whole point. 'Saved' conveys the idea of a person being rescued from some sort of desperate plight. This salvation includes conversion, commitment and 'professing', but cannot be reduced to any one of these terms. The idea of being saved from wrath, from the consequences of sin, has been lost in the polite re-wording of such offensive but thoroughly Biblical truth. The present day 'professing', to be found in such phrases as 'I professed myself', is the product of a much more radical change of thought, which has not only lost sight of the basic life-and-death issues involved when a man is born again, and brought out of darkness into light, but also makes the actions and its effects a human operation. The subject of the verb 'professed' is man; that of 'saved' is indubitably God.

The Gospel of Jesus Christ is the all-embracing story of the work of redemption accomplished by Christ on the cross of Calvary where he became our substitute, so that He could propitiate the wrath of God that we deserve as sinners. The Gospel is not a story that unfolds gradually, night after night, of a salvation that is mediated by workers and unless preached by them there is no hope of salvation.

Is there any hope that the 2x2 movement could make that mammoth leap from where it is today and turn to God in repentance and accept that where they stand, its workers preach what Paul calls 'another gospel.' The penalty for this is 'to be accursed' (Galatians 1:9).

What was the Gospel that Peter, Paul and the other apostles preached? They did not preach about a model of ministry instituted by Christ, or about the merits of a church that meets only in the home. Rather, they presented the message of salvation and expounded the things of 'first importance' as 1 Corinthians 15:3. This was that Christ died for our sins according to the Scriptures. A perusal of the sermons in Acts reveals that they all preached a message that was broadly similar. The message included the death and resurrection of Christ followed by a call to repentance.

In the words of Matt Chandler, 'we are saved, sanctified and sustained by what Jesus did for us on the cross. . . Romans 8:1 tells us that there is no condemnation for us, not because of all the great stuff we've done but because Christ has set us free from the law of sin and death. My sin in the past: forgiven. My current struggles: covered. My future failures: paid in full all by the marvellous, infinite, matchless grace found in the atoning work of the cross of Christ.'[450]

The 2x2 model of this ministry of preachers going out in pairs is by no means unique to the movement and is one of many models of ministry used to spread the Gospel of Jesus Christ. The church that meets in the home is a common practice amongst many Christian groups and if we return to the early days of Methodism in the eighteenth century we find that John Wesley encouraged this method of meeting. The 2x2 movement virtually excludes the death and resurrection of Jesus Christ and the sufficiency of the cross to atone for sin as the message. The emphasis is on the homeless ministry and on the church that meets in the home and this takes precedence over the apostolic pattern of preaching so evident in the Book of Acts.

The results of this investigation show certain deficiencies in the movement and how succeeding generations are misled into believing that they have a monopoly of 'the truth.' If a reader turns to the Bible with an open mind, forgetting the proof texts and asks the Holy Spirit for help, then He will convict of sin, righteousness and judgement,

---

[450] Chandler, Matt, *The Explicit Gospel*, (Nottingham: IVP, 2012), 15

(John 16:7-11). Salvation is a call to turn to Christ alone in repentance and be saved by grace through faith, 'and this is not your own doing, it is the gift of God, not a result of works so that no one may boast,' (Ephesians 2:8-9).

I contend that the message of the cross of Christ is the only means of salvation. In the words of Paul to the Corinthians, 'we implore you on behalf of Christ, be reconciled to God. For our sake he made him to be sin who knew no sin, so that in him we might become the righteousness of God' (2 Corinthians 5:20-21).

You may want to discuss this work with the author and you can do this in total confidence by emailing irvinegrey@yahoo.co.uk

Now I would remind you, brothers, of the gospel I preached to you, which you received, in which you stand, and by which you are being saved, if you hold fast to the word I preached to you - unless you believed in vain.

For I delivered to you as of first importance what I also received: that Christ died for our sins in accordance with the Scriptures, that he was buried, that he was raised on the third day in accordance with the Scriptures (1 Corinthians 15:1-4 ESV).